COURTING AT FIFTEEN.

MARRIED AT SEVENTEEN.

WOMEN

OF

NEW YORK.

Written and Illustrated

BY

MARIE LOUISE HANKINS,

Editress of the Pictorial "FAMILY NEWSPAPER," and Authoress of
"*Human Life;*" "*The Old Woman's Revenge;*" "*Bigamy;*"
"*The Bankrupt's Wife;*" "*Too Late;*"
"*The Needle Woman;*"
&c., &c., &c.

NEW-YORK:
MARIE LOUISE HANKINS & CO.
PUBLISHED AT THE
Office of Marie Louise Hankins' Pictorial "FAMILY NEWSPAPER."
1861.

THE AUTHORESS

OF

This Volume

RESPECTFULLY DEDICATES

IT TO ALL

INDUSTRIOUS AND WORTHY FEMALES,

Who have SPIRIT and PRIDE enough to honestly EARN THEIR OWN LIVING, instead of idly subsisting upon the

CHARITY AND BOUNTY

OF

RELATIVES AND FRIENDS

WHO ARE SOMETIMES

SCARCELY ABLE TO MAINTAIN THEMSELVES.

J. J. REED, PRINTER & STEREOTYPER,
43 & 45 Centre Street.

LA FARGE HOUSE, Broadway,
NEW YORK, Dec., 1860.

DEAR PUBLIC—

AGAIN I *bow* to you as the Authoress of a Book, and beg a few moments of your time by way of introduction. I do not ask an introduction for myself. I am well known to you already. It is my Book I wish to speak of. As Editress of the "Family Newspaper," and Contributor to other Periodicals, I salute you almost every day in the year, but I can afford to write a "full grown" Book only now and then. I'll be as brief as possible. I do not ask you to read a "PREFACE"—not I; for I well know that you have been pestered with such bores until you no longer have any patience with them. And I do not blame you, for *my* Editorial experience has given me a deep prejudice in that way. Instead of writing an odious "Preface," and expecting you to read it, I have thrown aside my pen, and put on my newest dress, from Lord and Taylor's, just finished in *the* latest style, by Madame Brackney, and otherwise arranged my toilet, so as to be "unexceptionably presentable," to even the most fastidious connoisseurs of taste and fashion. I do not fancy myself irresistible, but I have been at least an hour and a half in my dressing-room, before the mirror, with the assistance of Jenette, my waiting-maid, and as that is a third longer time than it generally requires to "get up" a fashionable lady for an evening party or a ball, I *think* no one will accuse me of not endeavoring to make myself look interesting. Jenette says, "Moi, M'lle Louise, how veeri sharming you do luke!" But then flattery is the finishing art of all French waiting-maids, and Jenette has learned it to perfection.

Well, thus attired in my best, and fully conscious of the insignificance of my humble self, I now stand before you, dear, kind, indulgent and amiable Public, and meekly bow my head for you to pass sentence. In my sanctum, quiet and alone, with only pen, ink and paper and my own thoughts to dwell upon, I was courageous and confident of success; but now my heart trembles; for beneath the gaze of so many thousand eyes, who could help feeling doubtful and timid? And *there* are those merciless *Critics*—"professional" in their way—who look at me sharply and scathingly, as though they would stare me *through*. At least one of them I know, and, yet, why should I fear *him?* He's nothing but a half-starved—well, no matter what he *is*, I'll just say that for reasons neither manly, right nor just, he

> "Applauds to-day what yesterday he curst,
> Lampoons the wisest, and extols the worst;
> While, hard to tell, so coarse a daub he lays,
> Which sullies most, his slander or his praise."

No: I'll not care a fig for him, nor any of his school. I write for the people. It is *you*, dear Public, I wish to please. So, let *demon* Critics avaunt! It requires a great deal of skill to please *everybody*, and it can hardly be expected that a Woman really possesses a sufficient quantum. However, I am well aware that modern readers, as a mass, prefer the newest and the most original, and I have therefore studied to make my book either remarkable or odd in every feature. Its name is certainly queer, and the sketches are all peculiar. It is "Original, Curious and *Truthful*," and may be read by the old and the young of both sex with profit and with pleasure. It is reasonable to expect that such a book will entertain more young folks than old; but if it is pleasant for many in the "sear and yellow leaf"

"To turn again their earlier volumes o'er,
And love them then because they've loved before;
And wily bless the waning hour that brings
A will to lean once more on single things,"

those in the wane of life who are tired of the bustling noise of the world, will also find by perusing these pages that

"'Tis pleasant, through the loopholes of retreat,
To peep at *such* a world: to see the stir
Of this great Babel, and not *feel* the crowd;
Nor *hear* the roaring din through all its streets,
At a snug distance, where the far off sound
Falls without a murmur on th' uninjur'd ear."

I have endeavored to make an *interesting* "book of the world," which shall abound with good and wholesome Common Sense Morality; and as there is a "home sermon" in almost every page, parents should first read it themselves and then place it in their daughter's hands.

But, dear Public, be kind enough to overlook the many blunders and imperfections you see; for an *original* book of this size, was never written and produced under similar circumstances and facilities, in so short a time. Will you believe it, when I tell you, that in six weeks from the day I began to write it, an edition of Ten Thousand copies were printed and bound complete? During that short time I had many, many other things to attend to, and the dear knows how much *other* writing to do, and these Sketches were prepared "piece meal," in the moments I could spare. I had no time to revise and improve the MSS., and with so much haste, the result cannot be as perfect as it should have been. Yet, dear Public, if *you* will buy and read, and then merely say, " 'Twill *do*," I shall be contented.

> " But be not long, for in the tedious minutes,
> Exquisite interval, I'm on the rack."

And all this for a little FAME. I'll confess the truth. If it were not for Profit and Fame, one or the other, or *both* together, very few writers would toil as they do. Everybody knows the end of " Profit"—for 'tis their *bread and butter*. But in the words of the poet,

> " What is the end of 'Fame' ? 'Tis but to fill
> A certain portion of uncertain paper ;
> Some liken it to climbing up a hill,
> Whose summit, like *all* hills, is lost in vapor.
> For *this* men write, speak, preach, and heroes kill,
> And bards burn what *they* call ' the midnight taper.' "

I am, dear Public, your most obedient servant,

MARIE LOUISE HANKINS,

Editress of the " FAMILY NEWSPAPER."

PROLOGUE.

TO WOMAN ON EARTH.

EARTH ! Thou would'st be a blank, a dreary waste,
A mighty desert without aught to cheer,
If lovely Woman were not ever near,
To bless Man's home with comfort and with taste.

* * * * * *

I saw her in her gladsome *childhood*,
When her smiles to all were dear,
And her laughter through the wild wood
Rang like bird-notes light and clear,
As she with her baby brother
Gambol'd through the summer day;
While the eyes of a fond mother
Watched them in their merry play.
Then I whispered gently, "Lovebird,
Tell me—dost thou wish to die?"
And she, like a startled dove, heard
The dread words with frighted eye.
"*Die?*" she said; "the word's so dreary!
Leave my brother—friends—my flowers?
Name it not! I am not weary—
'Tis so fair, this world of ours!"

Years pass'd on—a beauteous maiden's
Form eclipsed the child's of yore;
Now her words with sweeter cadence
Trembled, and her deep eyes wore
A lovelier light: a glorious being,
In his manhood's richest prime,
Wandered by her side, naught seeing
Save one face: sweet summer time!
Then again the words I breathed,—
"Canst thou now the world deny?
Are the flowers of earth still wreathed
Round about thee?—canst thou die?"
How her heart, that heart that won *him*,
Trembled:—to be calm she strove—
Turned her tearful eyes upon him,
Murmuring, "Not yet! *I love!*"

Again years passed—all former gladness
With them from her heart had fled;

Clad in mourning robes of sadness,
  Sat she grieving for the dead.
One sweet babe her arms enfolded,
  In a mother's own embrace,
And the vision fair seemed moulded
  From her long-lost childhood's face.
Eyes with love and sorrow beaming,
  As once more I asked, "Couldst die?"
Then with eager answer gleaming—
  "Oh, might I by *his* side *now* lie!
Earthly joys are false and *hollow;*
  'Tis not much the world can give:
He has gone—I fain would follow—
  Nay! still *for my child* I'll live!"

Once again I saw her—sorrow
  Long had dimmed her eye so bright—
Waiting, watching for the morrow—
  Auburn tresses streaked with white.
Then I saw her softly stealing,
  In the twilight's dusky shade,
To the churchyard; saw her kneeling
  Where her darling child was laid.
Autumn winds were sadly sighing,
  Seeming for some boon to crave;
Autumn leaves were drooping, dying,
  Fading on that tiny grave.
Once again the words were spoken—
  "Is it now the time to die?"
"*It is*—I go, in accents broken,
  "I join my loved ones in the sky!"

* * * * *

Ah, Woman! what were life *without* thy love?
  Thou, whom our Maker formed so fair,
  One would believe—thy beauty is so rare—
Thee an angel sent hither from above.

Prologue.

Should a man be with sorrow opprest,
  Thou, woman, his care will beguile;
By his sick-bed thou'lt watch without rest
  His labors will cheer with a smile

And should poverty, nay, even shame,
  Reach him who has once gained thy heart,
Thou'lt continue to love on the same,
  Though all else unkindly depart.

For, the love that *true* woman bestows,
  Though lowly her lot may be cast,
Entwined with her life as it grows,
  Is constant, and ever will last.

Then *to* man, O, woman, be very *dear!*
  Be cherish'd with *honor* and *love;*
For, though man may to man be sincere,
  Thou, always, his *best* friend will prove.

Thy holy mission is man's path to cheer,
  To comfort him whene'er in care and strife,
  And ever while he lives to make his life,
His home, to him a thousand-fold more dear;
May'st thou thy mission well fulfill, and *he*
Never *neglect* that which is *due* to THEE!

SYNOPSIS

OF

PORTRAITS AND CHARACTERS.

MANY YEARS AGO.

IN THE YEAR 1860.

WOMEN OF NEW YORK

PECULIARITIES TO BEGIN WITH.

Oh, woman! subtle, lovely, faithless sex!
Born to enchant, thou studiest to perplex.—Paine

Oh! frail inconstancy of mortal state!
One hour dejected and the next elate!—Pattison.

Vain human kind! fantastic race
Thy various follies who can trace?—Swift.

'Tis pity tho', in this sublime world, that
Pleasure's a sin, and sometimes sin's a pleasure.—Byron.

BY "*Women* of New York," we mean females in general who inhabit the metropolis. If the *men* of New York are peculiar, the women are more so. It is said that women are all *alike* the world over, but the New York female is a most wonderful study for moral philosophers and readers of human nature.

The strong throbbing of the city's busy heart, like the beating of that within every human breast, influences the most remote and insignificant members. As the cessation of that constant beating which counts each second of our brief existence, would cause our senses to fail us and our hands to drop forever motionless, so the pausing of New York's commercial bosom, (were such a thing possible,) would involve in ruin the humble mechanic and the petty dealer in rags and bones, as well as the merchant whose interest is vested in a hundred ships. The activity, the prosperity, the restless struggle for wealth and precedence, which has been going on for years within the great metropolis, seems to have created a type of mortals fitted to breathe its atmosphere, and endure its bustle. They are well worth a few glances of attention and a few words of praise and censure.

Thus, readers, for your benefit, we raise the curtain upon the busy scene, unroof the palace of the millionaire and the hovel of the poor—thus mount to the dismantled attic, and then peep behind the curtains of the luxurious *boudoir*, revealing what we can of the life and habits of the weaker sex, in various ranks and stations, without one word which will shock the ears of the most fastidious, or one picture which a judicious parent need fear to place before the eyes of her innocent daughter.

The scenes and events in these pages have been " drawn from real life," and perhaps some acute masculine, who imagines that *one* woman he chances to know, is a type of all her sex, may here learn the fallacy of his opinions and receive the idea that women *can* be spoken of collectively in a respectful manner.

A woman may be either a blessed comforter, a sympathizing friend, a silly doll, a selfish leech, or an edged tool, to the man with whom she is related by the ties of daughter, wife or sister. And New York women go to the extreme of good or bad in whichever position they may stand. Find a more perfect specimen of her sex than a virtuous New York lady, descended perhaps, from the old Knickerbocker stock, handsome, graceful, accomplished, and well read, fitted by habits and associations for companionship with the greatest upon earth, and in every domestic relation, a pattern to the present and to future generations. Look, then, upon the other side. Can there be a more intensely vulgar, ignorant, prejudiced, wicked and remorseless creature, than a " low" New York female? Is there more superlative vulgarity of speech, dress and manners, to be found any where in the world? Her mate cannot be found. And so in the middle classes. The mechanic's wife is more emphatically a mechanic's wife. You can almost tell the doctor's spouse, or the minister's help-mate, without an introduction. Economical people are doubly economical, extravagant people triply extravagant, good people excessively good, and bad people outrageously wicked, while selfish people, (oh what shoals there are of these upon life's waters,) are grasping and forgetful of all interests save their own.

Now let us see whither we are about to go, and upon what we are to gaze during the course of our journey. In old times, when Pearl street was "up town," and people moved to localities now devoted to wholesale purposes, for "fresh air for the children," we would have had a smaller field to traverse, and quite different things to relate. With the growth of Gotham the vices and the business of its inhabitants have increased ten fold.

Behold the women of whom we are about to write! The humblest among them has at least an aspiration to greater magnificence of toilette, than would have contented the wealthiest of our great grand mothers. Where will you now find the well preserved "best dress,"—the silk worn Sabbath after Sabbath for ten or twenty years,—the shawl which is a family heir-loom, or the old velvet mantle, which for generations have made a show? Where is the servant girl who wears a costume adapted to her duties and position in life, or who would mark herself as a menial by the assumption of the style enforced eighty years ago upon every domestic? A skirt and jacket, "sheperdess," the last was called, which differed in make and material diametrically from the "robe," or "gown," worn by the lady mistress. On the contrary, the washerwoman's Sunday attire is now as nearly like that of the merchant's wife as it can be, and the bootblack's daughter wears a bonnet made like that of the Empress of the French. All women's backs are alike, to those who are not posted in the prices and qualities of dry goods. There is now very little difference in comparison with the varied incomes of the women who promenade our streets.

A New York woman will seldom own that she is poor or unfashionable, until she absolutely suffers destitution. But the destitute are many. It is frightful to think how numerous they are. Our asylums and our public institutions, are filled to overflowing. Yet, alas! the damp hovel, the tottering tenement house, even the corners of empty cellars, the niches of new buildings, and piles of boards or barrels, shelter myriads of starving, shivering, hopeless mortals, every night.

Among the women who thus suffer for their own or others thriftlessness or crime, none can be found who began life as they will end it. In the homes of wealth, there are very few who were born to the enjoyment of luxury.

The wheel of fortune turns no where so swiftly as in the great metropolis. New Yorkers *must* go up or down, must sink or swim. They make fortunes in a year, or lose them in a day. A friendly push sends some to the top of the see-saw, an unlucky jounce precipitates others head long to the bottom. You cannot crawl up two feet and back one, in Gotham's slippery road. It is either the top or the bottom, towards which we are always progressing. All the better for the lucky ones, and all the worse for those who fall. It is impossible to tell the future life of the child, by the circumstances in which fate appears to have placed it. Make the attempt, and you will soon see your mistake.

Perhaps the principal cause of the rapid approach of want and misery to women reared in ease and plenty, and then thrown upon their own resources, is the idleness in which they are almost universally educated. A fashionable lady is as helpless with her hands, as a

Chinese woman is with her feet. Her delicate fingers are shapely and white it is true, but they are not capable of providing the common necessaries of life, for even one human being. To sew, to make bread, to sweep or wash, would be to degrade herself. To learn a trade or profession, with which, if necessary, she might support existence, would be a drudgery she could not contemplate for a moment. Then her education is superficial, and her accomplishments, even should she be talented, are merely dabbled in, not learned. She can sing, play, paint flowers, and perhaps write poetry —but *only* "a little." She is seldom mistress of any one art, sufficiently to enable her to adopt it as a profession. Her beauty alone, has been well nourished and cared for; and from girlhood, her constant object has been marriage. Once the wife of an eligible suitor, she expects to be supported in a sumptuous style, until her dying day. Should death deprive her of her protector, leaving her unexpectedly penniless, she has no power to struggle with her destiny, but sinks inertly, unless some kind friend or relation proffers his charity. The unfledged bird, the babe of a brief week's existence, is as strong a thing as many a full grown fashionable lady, left to her own resources.

Now and then, sensible people among the wealthy classes give their daughters the power to be independent, by encouraging their talent, or instructing them in some art, by which they might, if necessiated, gain a livelihood. But such common sense is rare. And thus it is that we continually see the poor mount, and the rich fall.

The servant has the use of her fingers, and never need to starve. The milliner, ready to seize at bargains, and turn a penny by some change in the prevailing mode, can make a fortune. The shop keeper's wife is his best aid behind the counter, and by slow degrees each attains a position above that in which she began life. Starting in a shanty, may end in a palace. Yet having once attained an eminence, these very people deny their children the advantages which made them what they are. Believing idleness a mark of superiority, they educate their offspring to an inaction, which degrades both mind and body, renders the girls mere walking fashion plates, and causes the boys to become the dissipated idlers, who will inevitably run through any fortune, and bring themselves and their sisters to beggary.

Women, think of this! Read the various experiences herein presented, and profit therefrom.

RUTH MARTIN

RUTH MARTIN:

THE SPIRITUAL MEDIUM.

"I can call up spirits from the vasty deep!"
"Why so can I, or so can any man!"
"But will they come, when you do call for them?"—SHAKS.

THE picture of poor Ruth is a veritable portrait, and the type of a class who have sprung up, mushroom-like, in our midst.

There are charlatans among the professors of spiritualism, who for the sake of gain play upon the credulity of those visiting them. Men and women who disguise the basest intentions beneath the cloak of superstition, and poor dupes, who are either the tools of those about them, or the victims of their own morbid imagination and warped intellect. To this last order belongs Ruth Martin, a woman who was but a few years ago lovely, loved, and loving. This prevailing madness has torn health and happiness forever from her. Many a husband will sigh as he reads this; many a father and brother, aye ! many a son and daughter will sadly think of some dear one, either already sunk, or fast sinking into the mire of spiritual mania. For, alas, how many wives, sisters, daughters and mothers, have been degraded by its blackness.

Ruth Martin, at sixteen, was as pretty and sweet a girl as could be found among the first circles of our society. No pains had been spared upon her education, and in the solid branches, as well as every lady-like accomplishment, she was well versed and brilliant. The only noticable fault in her personal appearance, was the want of color ; and the only point which marred her character, was a disposition to melancholy. Small, plump, and fair as an infant, this personal defect was rarely commented upon ; and as for the mental peculiarity, a life of uninterrupted ease was not calculated for its development. Her melancholy found its outlet in sentimental songs, and touching incidents in plays and novels, and seldom, or never, intruded itself upon the daily recurrences of her existence.

At eighteen, Ruth formed an attachment for a young and handsome man, who had long loved her fondly, and she was betrothed to him with the full consent of her parents. The wedding day was fixed, the wedding garments fashioned, and even the ring lay waiting to encircle her finger, when death, as though envious of so much happiness, raised its scythe and cut down the young lover in the very summer of his life. On the morning of the day which should have witnessed their nuptials, he died in Ruth's arms, and with him perished all the hope and youth of the young girl's existence. From the long illness which followed this dreadful shock, she arose the faded wreck of her former self in mind and person. Just at this time, the spiritual fever was beginning to spread. There were "manifestations" here, and "mediums" there. You read, in each morning's paper, of children, scarcely old enough to speak, who had communication with the invisible world; of ignorant men who, in "the trance state," penned erudite essays on scientific subjects; and of tables and chairs, becoming capable of volition, on the application of the tips of certain gifted fingers.

Ruth heard these rumors, and was fascinated by them. The beautiful idea, that we are watched over by guardian angels, lingers in every pure Christian heart; and Ruth treasured this hope as a miser does his gold. To hear from her dead lover; to know that in the world beyond Death's mystic river, he waited for her coming; to be assured that, in that higher sphere, we love and are beloved, as upon earth, was her constant prayer by night and day, and the charlatans, who live upon the folly of the credulous, found her an easy prey.

At first the delusion was at times apparent even to Ruth's warped mind. She felt that the "manifestations" were vague and pointless, and that jugglery might be the cause of the effects she witnessed; but, after a little while, the clouds gathered more closely about her, and all she saw seemed of divine origin. Bye and bye she began to believe herself endowed with the power of communicating with beings of another world. She saw visions—heard heavy blows upon the wall—felt her hand seized in the cold clasp of unseen fingers, and in fact, was subject to all those terrible and unaccountable delusions which take possession of the votaries of spiritualism. Hitherto, she had been as docile and obedient to her parents as a child; but now, their tears and remonstrances aroused her anger. She regarded them as obstacles between herself and some great good, and gradually weaned herself from their care and protection, and sought companions who encouraged or participated in her delusion. The last years of her old father's life were spent in vain endeavors to guard his daughter from the evil effects of her insanity.

and her weary mother died of a broken heart, soon after following her husband to the grave. They left property behind them, and this became poor Ruth's. Now, indeed, was the unhappy woman in peril. Her new made friends gathered more closely around her ; the dear old home, which had sheltered her innocent childhood, became the scene of midnight orgies. What otherwise would still have been revolting in the extreme, became tolerable when she believed it "done under the direction of the spirits ;" and, at length, her fair fame was tarnished by the conduct and character of those with whom she had become identified. At last, she herself—she, who had once been so pure and spotless, faltered, and fell. Among her associates, there was one who hid the heart and propensities of a tiger beneath a sanctimonious exterior. His face was expressionless ; but you could read in his cold, glittering, grey eye, a subtle cunning and determination which would enable him to accomplish any purpose, and overcome any obstacle. Above all he had that peculiar mesmeric power, which is sometimes found in men of strong and active minds, and which can compel those of weak bodies and vascilating dispositions to almost involuntary obedience. Ruth was rich. Money was the engine which this man most lacked and needed. Her delusion favored him in his schemes, and, like a bird of prey, he hovered above his victim, gradually diminishing the circles of his flight, and drawing near her by imperceptible degrees. He spoke first of affinity. He bewildered her by doctrines specious as they were vile, and, finally, brought advice, which suited his purpose, from the lips of other mediums in whom poor Ruth placed implicit reliance. In addition to all this, he was very kind, and so few were sincerely kind to the lonely woman. Sometimes too, when they were alone, he whispered words of love and flattery, sweet always to any woman's ear, and they fell very soothingly upon Ruth's weary heart. At first she only listened to them: bye and bye she began to crave them, and in a little while she was his, to be played with for a brief space, then tortured, robbed, and deserted. When he had obtained all that his credulous victim possessed, he left her, almost penniless, to support existence as best she might. She never heard of him again. The designing comrades, who surrounded her in her days of plenty, left her in her poverty: and in this last misery, the mania which first misled her, now grew even more powerful. She saw departed ones standing beside her—heard mysterious warnings in the air—foretold the future, and spoke in unknown tongues. A circle of believers gathered about her, listening with awe to her incoherent rhapsodies, and believing her inspired when her warped mind caused her to assume the mien and language of a prophetess. For a while Spiritualists spoke of her as "the best living Medium," and the uninitiated laughed or marvelled according to their gifts of mirth, or credulity. But the end was coming.

One cold winter evening, when happy families gathered about their blazing hearths, and there was mirth and joy and music in many a home where Ruth had once been a loved and welcome guest, the poor creature, now banished from virtues's dwelling places, was the center of a circle, composed of believers and strangers, whom curiosity had attracted to the spot. The demon was at work within her, and all the mystic manifestations were at their height. Those who had seen Ruth frequently, were now astonished by the brightness of her wild sunken eyes, and they noticed that a spot of vivid crimson burned upon her cheeks, which were usually colorless as those of a corpse. All was quiet. The believers were eagerly awaiting the next manifestation from their prophetess, who sat with her head bowed upon her bosom, and the sceptics were growing sleepy or impatient.

Suddenly, without a sign of warning, Ruth arose, and seizing a burning lamp, she threw it with an unearthly scream in the midst of the affrighted congregation. In an instant, the room was cleared. The horrified spectators rushed wildly down the creaking stairs and into the open air, and after them, with blood-shot eyes, disordered hair, and frantic jestures, darted a maniac, foaming at the mouth, and uttering shrieks which made the blood of strong men curdle in their veins. The last spark of reason had fled from poor Ruth's disordered mind, never to be rekindled more.

In an asylum, where other poor insane creatures are cared for, or neglected, at the public expense, you may now see poor Ruth's hollow cheeks and vacant eyes, and, in her more quiet moments, may hear her speak of spirits who are beckoning to her from beyond the grated windows. And spirits *are* calling her. In a little while the disfigured clay will be laid beneath the earth, and the soul, restored and purified, will return again to Him who gave it.

MAGGIE BREWER.

MAGGIE BREWER:

THE MILLINER'S GIRL.

But then her face,
So lovely, yet so arch—so full of mirth,
The overflowing of an innocent heart.—ROGERS.

AGGIE Brewer is all day alternating between the shop and the room back of it, selling bonnets, flowers and feathers in the one, and stitching "for dear life," in the other. Never, on any account, looking dull or stupid, or forgetting the fact that she is an exceedingly pretty girl.

Old Mrs. Stitchem, the proprietess of the establishment, declares that Maggie is worth fifty other shop girls, and Miss Betsy, the forewoman, had rather have her services than those of any of her assistants. As for the ladies who patronize Mrs. Stitchem, they are equally well pleased, for Maggie is never weary of looking for "just this shade of blue," or "just that width of ribbon," and will disembowel fifty boxes for the benefit of their curiosity, without a single murmur. Many and many a young man, allured within the glass doors, by the pretty face behind the counter, and, intending to spend nothing, has found his pockets lighter by several dollars, and his hands full of gauzy nothings, of which he could make no possible use—for Maggie is a thorough little tradeswoman, and uses her smiles and beauty as well as she does her nimble fingers. She can flirt in the most approved manner, and is as wicked a coquette as can be found upon this mundane sphere ; but, as far as real virtue is concerned, she is incorruptible, and would guard her honor with her very life.

Maggie is quick of speech, and can express herself fluently, but her grammar is somewhat deficient, and she is fond of a superfluity of negatives. Any thing she disapproves of, is stigmatised as "real mean." Over-work is "real mean," bad needles are "real mean," and *scolding* is "real mean." A rainy day, or too fastidious customers—a rent in her best dress, or a bad dinner, all are "*real* mean." There is no stronger term in her vocabulary. Maggie's dress, on holidays, is as scrupulously arranged as that of any Fifth Avenue belle. Her bonnet, with its gay flowers, shades the glossiest of ringlets, and her long skirts sweep the sidewalk with as great a disregard of economy as though she was worth a million. A shabby garment is the only thing which will give Maggie a fit of the blues, and a badly fitting basque is the object of her supreme and unlimited disgust.

Maggie's home is situated on the "East side" of New York, beyond the Bowery, in one of the streets running down towards the river, and there she dwells, in company with her widowed mother and several sisters, who are either dressmakers or tailoresses. The young men of the neighborhood cast glances of admiration on Maggie, as she goes toward the shop in the early morning ; and the butcher around the corner is driven to distraction's verge by the prejudice which old Mrs. Brewer entertains against him.

One of Maggie's sisters is engaged to a prosperous journeyman tailor, and the others have each "their young man," who is supposed to be paying "particular attention," by all the watchful observers. But, in general, she passes to and fro without disturbance, thinking of all those objects of interest which the humblest life affords, or calculating (if it be Saturday night) how far the little sum in her portemonaie can be made to go ; and on the whole is perhaps as happy as many a richer maiden, who rolls past her among the cushioned seats of their father's carriages. During her shopping excursions, Maggie patronizes the Bowery. There the colors are brighter, the patterns larger, and the clerks more loqucious. There are bargains to be met with. Damaged lace at less than cost, veils from auction, at half price, pink lilies and blue roses, to be purchased for a mere song, and embroidered cotton handkerchiefs, which the shopmen declare can never be told from linen, for a shilling a piece.

It is Maggie's delight to visit these stores by gaslight, in company with several young women of her acquaintance, and then and there expend all her superfluous cash in the purchase of various articles of adornment, and go home chatting about that "real pretty clerk who measured the ribbon," or that "real *mean* man who would not throw off sixpence on the muslin." Another great enjoyment is to be escorted in the evening, by some spruce young beau, to an ice cream saloon, and there to be refreshed with various delicacies, and overwhelmed with attentions. Other girls are there to observe and admire, and other beaus to grow jealous. There is always such a pretty fountain in the centre, with a white statue throwing water over its head, and such a nice display of artificial flowers, and the waiters, in their white aprons, are as polite as though they were serving a princess. Indeed, Maggie quite imagines herself a great lady, and draws off her kid gloves with an air. Going home, they always walk slowly, and are disposed to talk sentimentally. The young man says, he " would have like to have stayed in that there place for a considerable time." And the young lady inquires " Why ?" And her escort answers, " 'Cause he had such good company." This brings a brighter red to her cheek, and she turns away from him. Then, somehow, Maggie finds herself looking out of her little attic window, long after she ought to be asleep, wondering " whether he really meant anything by it," and imagining the feelings of a bride, in white attire and orange flowers. Some of these bright evenings there will be more smiles and blushes, and a strong palpitation of a certain good, honest heart ; and after that, Maggie will " keep regular company," and will have lovers' quarrels, and make them up again ; and, finally, she will get married, and settle down as wife and mother, in some compact little second or third floor. Such a time as they will have at the wedding defies description. All the relatives and friends will be invited. Sarah's young man, and Lizzie's young man, will come, of course ; and there will be a plentiful feast prepared for their entertainment. The rich old aunt, from Peekskill, will bring a present of teaspoons, and will make Maggie blush by whispering to her, that "in a year she will also give her a cradle." The bridesmaid will have to endure sundry jokes, about bridesmaids being always destined for brides, in the shortest space of time. And the sisters will be informed, by all the old ladies, that *their* turn is coming next. All the gentlemen will salute the bride, and try to kiss the bridesmaids; and there will be much screaming, and running into corners, and the ugliest damsel will be far the easiest to capture. And after supper, there will be a good deal of singing, and a number of tunes upon the somewhat cracked piano-forte, and as much dancing as can be managed in the limited space between the table and the fireplace; and a little after midnight, the guests will take their departure, and Maggie Brewer will bid them adieu as "*Mrs. Smith.*"

If Maggie's husband is prosperous, she may some day move from the second floor to a brown stone mansion, and, perhaps, eventually keep her carriage, and a dozen servants. Should you meet her after she gets up in the world, you will recognize her by some lapses in grammar, and a habit of wearing very gay flowers in her bonnet. But, although neither refined nor edücated, she will still have the same light spirit, gay heart, and nimble fingers, as when she measured ribbon for Mrs. Stitchem; and although she may be sneered at "for having risen from nothing," and looked upon with ridicule by some of her more well born neighbors; she will be very happy, and make a loving wife, and good mother.

But Maggie Brewer is better off than the great multitude of shop girls in New York. Maggie has a *home* where she can live with a good, kind mother, and in the companionship of her sisters and little brother. She receives nine dollars a week for her services in the shop of Mrs. Stitchem, while her co-laborers get only three or four.

There is a mischievous spirit governing the will and actions of all working females. They seem to cherish the idea, that being women, they should live without labor. From infancy up, they are continually counting upon assistance and support from relations or friends, or looking forward to the time when they shall have a husband to provide for their wants.

It is frequently said, that in New York, there is nothing for working females to do; or that the compensation they receive is not adequate to their wants. How could it be otherwise, when there is such a total lack of care or concern, on the part of the operative females, towards the interest of their employers. They work only for their wages, and anxiously watch the clock for the hour to quit. They submit to it spitefully, and only for the time being, expecting, of course, to drop it to-morrow or next week, and fly into some harbor of rest,—some haven of repose, where their wants must be provided for, and where luxuries shall be showered about them. And such is the feeling of shop girls generally. No wonder then, that their employers can not pay them more. It would be unreasonable to reward their assistants for inattention and neglect. Maggie Brewer is an exception to the masses, and consequently she receives a fair compensation. Some get even higher wages, but they are still more competent and useful, and increase the profit of their employers, where others would carelessly let in waste and destruction. If shop girls acted upon the same principle that men are obliged to, they would be worth far more to their employers, and feel a thousand times happier themselves.

ANGELINA PLUMP.

ANGELINA PLUMP:

THE LAP DOG'S MOTHER.

Leave her to heaven,
And to those thorns that in her bosom lodge,
To prick and sting her!

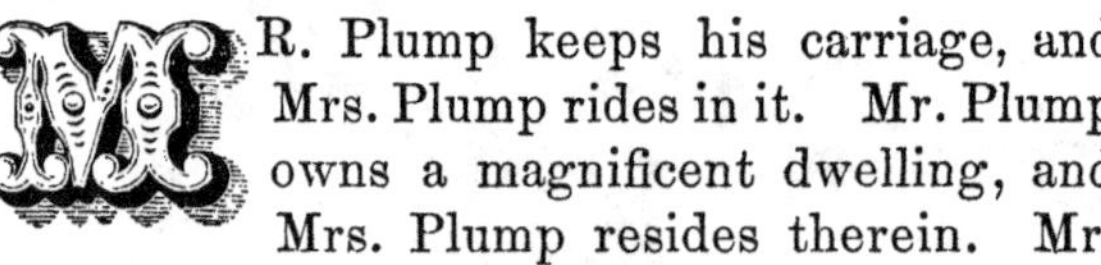
R. Plump keeps his carriage, and Mrs. Plump rides in it. Mr. Plump owns a magnificent dwelling, and Mrs. Plump resides therein. Mr. Plump has purchased chairs, tables, sofas, beds, and carpets, of the most splendid kind and quality, and Mrs. Plump sits upon, eats off of, lolls over, sleeps in, and walks over said articles. It is a man's duty to provide such luxuries for his wife, and it is the province of a woman to enjoy them. Mrs. Plump cannot imagine that she has another earthly obligation. At the altar she promised to love, honor, and obey Mr. Plump, with the idea that the vow signified only her willingness to dwell in his mansion, eat off his china and silver, and allow him to pay her milliner's bills. And in her daily con-

versation, she alludes to herself, not as the wife of Mr. Plump, or the parent of their only child, but she styles herself "Fido's Ma." Fido is a little dog, white, curly, red-eyed, and spiteful. He is washed every day, combed and curled as regularly as a dandy's moustache, and embellished with a blue ribbon and gold buckle in summer, and by a little crimson blanket in winter. Mrs. Plump always takes Fido out with her when she drives down Broadway to Lord & Taylor's, and her maid goes along to carry the sweet animal behind his mistress when she alights. Mrs. Plump often electrifies the pedestrians by screaming in sentimental tones, whenever her favorite whines aloud—

"Bless its little heart,—did Fido want to come to his ma?"

Meanwhile, the lady's own child is leaning from the nursery window, or pleads in vain with the lazy nurse, for a walk in the garden, or to the square. Poor child! "Fido's Ma" would not be seen with an infant on her knee for Queen Victoria's crown and scepter; and she sometimes passes whole days without even visiting her little son in the nursery.

"Jones!" Mrs. Plump will remark to nurse; "Jones, is your young master dressed in his claret colored velvet?"

"Yes, ma'am," replies the girl, whose christian name is Ann, but who is always spoken to as 'Jones,' because great people in England sometimes address their servants in this wise, and Mrs. Plump apes the manners of the foreign nobility, "Yes, ma'am, and his little gold armlets."

"Well, and you'r sure his hair looks nicely, Jones!" continues her mistress.

"Yes, ma'am. I fixed it with my own two hands!"

"Then, Jones, if Miss Wilcox calls, let him come into the parlor for five minutes; but otherwise don't allow him to disturb me, for my nerves won't stand his noise, and poor, dear Fido is not well to-day."

Nurse courtesies and retires, and little Charley is "not allowed to disturb his mamma" that day nor the next, while Mr. Plump, immersed in speculation, seldom remembers that he has a son, and the servants, as selfish as their superiors, are always too busy or too cross, to humor the child's innocent wishes.

Mrs. Plump calls, and shops, and receives visits, and attends parties and balls, and goes to the opera. Her spouse spends his mornings among the speculators of Wall-street, and finishes his day anywhere rather than at home, for his wife is only "Fido's ma," and neither wishes for nor misses his society. Now and then they give a grand party, and the lady and gentleman are both present. The tables are spread with costly delicacies, and the rooms are full of rich and fashionable people. Music and ill-natured remarks, dancing and scandal, cards and envy, pass away the night, and the guests compliment the host and hostess, and go away to whisper —that " this can't last long, and that there will be a failure one of these days." And these gatherings are the sum total of the domestic comfort or hospitality with which this fashionable mansion is acquainted. There seems to be no link between the hearts of its selfish occupants. The husband fills his establishment with costly furniture, and clothes his wife in velvet and diamonds, as though he were paying a debt of long standing, incurred for something he had never valued. The wife enjoys her luxuries, because they were her object in marrying. The child is dressed to match the other appointments of the household, and fed, because it is fashionable to feed one's children. He was christened more to exhibit his costly embroidered robe than for any higher purpose, and will in a few years be sent to boarding-school to get him out of the way. How the boy will grow up, or what kind of a man he will become, it is impossible to imagine. Certainly he will never feel the holy restraint of a happy home and loving parents, when he is tempted to wickedness or folly. He can never remember a father's counsel, nor a mother's kisses. He was cared for by servants in his infancy ; and in his manhood, will scarcely turn to seek those who were almost strangers to him when a child. In all probability he will be wild and heartless, and will anticipate, with unnatural joy, the hour which shall make him sole possessor of his father's wealth, while for his mother he will entertain neither reverence nor love. How could he love his mother, when throughout his boyhood he cannot remember her as his friend and counselor, nor as the one who smiled upon his worthy acts, and wept when he did wrong, nor as the tender guardian in whom most boys find their safeguard from temptation, but only as a heartless, brainless doll, a piece of rouged and ringletted affectation, calling itself with a simper—" Fido's ma." How could he love such a mother?

If the census taker had been permitted to return us the names of all the Mrs. Plumps who live in the city, no doubt we should have raised our hands in wonder to know how many *fashionable* mothers, prefer petting lap dogs, to bestowing natural love and duty upon their own offspring. We feel safe in saying that there are at this moment thousands of innocent little Harries, Johnies, and Charlies, and Jennies, Carries and Lizzies, between the ages of three months and ten years, and of rich parents, weeping and crying under the cold, hired attention of nurses who come to New York from Great Britain, on purpose to take care of children ; and we can conclude with equal certainty that the parents of these hapless children are absent somewhere in gay pursuit of their personal pleasure, and would not pause to answer the imploring cry of "pa," or "ma." One would infer that it must be unnatural for a mother to love her child, when she hides it away and employs a stranger to perform her duty for her, while she adopts a sickly, sore-eyed poodle, to nurse and carry about, instead. We have frequently sighed in compassion, for the ragged children of destitution and want as they pass us shivering, in the thoroughfares, and have sometimes felt more than half like crying to think what will become of them ; but upon sober reflection we feel more doubtful concerning the destiny of the child of the rich lady who glories in calling herself a *lap dog's mother*.

MRS. BIFFLES.

MRS. BIFFLES.

THE PHILANTHROPIST.

And *Justice* while she winks at crimes
Stumbles on innocence sometimes.—BUTLER.

RS. Biffles is a good old lady, who was born somewhere in the State of Massachusetts. Her father was a Baptist minister, and her mother a lady of the practical school, who did not believe in laughter, music, children's pastime, nor other frivolous methods of wasting hours which might be devoted to paring apples or studying the catechism.

Little Sarah was early taught to sit up straight, knit stockings, and go to church three times every Sunday. She never skipped the rope, nor rolled the hoop, nor played at battledoor and shuttlecock, nor " ring around a rosy." In her blue checked apron and brown merino dress, she was a little old woman, demure and solemn.

As she grew older, her mind was developed by the perusal of the biographies of departed children, who were all perfection during their life time, and this course of study was now and then relieved by the lives and wanderings of missionaries, who had narrowly escaped being devoured by cannibals, or being thrown as sacrifices to some Hindoo idol, who was supposed to be greatly aggrieved by their unwelcome presence. Once the poor child sat down under the shadow of the old grape-vine to dream over Scott's Ivanhoe, an old copy of which she had found hidden upon an upper shelf of a cupboard in the attic, but in the midst of her enjoyment the volume was whisked away by the hands of her watchful mother, and she was led forthwith to her father's study, to be accused of the flagrant crime of "*reading novels.*"

Thus prevented from indulging her tastes in literature, poor Sarah conceived an aversion for books, and turned her attention to human nature, determining to become a philanthropist, and like Don Quixote, redress the grievances of the world. She began with the poor of her own neighborhood, and endeavored persistently to make them all go to church. But after a drunken cobbler had chased her down the road, with a hot poker in his hand, for meddling in his domestic affairs, and she had caught the scarlet fever, by visiting a family where the children were just suffering from an attack of that dire disease, she refrained from this attempt, and turned her thoughts towards the culprits in prison. They, poor fellows, could not resent any interference, and under the impression that she was a second Mrs. Fry, the good Sarah visited the Frogtown jail three times every week, bearing in her reticule a large supply of tracts and moral essays. She had a promising set of pupils. There was Dick Dangle, the drunken vagrant, who had led a life of sottish dissipation for over sixty years, and who always put an abrupt end to the young lady's harangue by remarking—

"Yes, yes—*that's* very true, and you have a deal of learning, but I'm not young enough to begin them things, and if yer would only give me a sixpence to buy a drop of whisky to keep the cold out of my stomach, you'd be doing me a great kindness."

A young thief, who made faces behind her back, a woman who had robbed a dwelling-house, and who always made a point of going to sleep the moment Miss Sarah entered, and from ten to fifteen minor offenders, who had committed assault and battery, or stolen apples or turkeys—all confined on charges of vagrancy, completed the list. How long the young woman would have continued her efforts it is impossible to say, for at the age of eighteen, she married a small man by the name of Biffles, and removed with him to New York. For a few years her philanthropic efforts were at rest.

Mrs. Biffles filled her thoughts and occupied her hands, but as they grew older, all the fervor of her disposition broke out in a fresh direction, and she became the "friend of the oppressed slave." She prayed for him, wept for him, and lectured about him. She was for freeing the whole mass of southern negroes in one day, and allowing them to run pell-mell over the United States, to earn their own subsistence by white-washing, or starve to death, just as it might happen, so long as they enjoyed a "glorious freedom," which only one out of twenty could possibly appreciate. She attended abolition meetings, made speeches, called the southerners hard names, screamed for aid for "the crushed and oppressed mulatto," and advised freemen "to arm in aid of their enslaved brethren."

Meanwhile her own dwelling was neglected. Her children grew up like weeds, and Mr. Biffles seldom had buttons on his linen. Many and many a night did that much injured man wait with an umbrella in the lobby of some lecture-room, while the tones of his wife's loud voice were still ringing upon the air, and the neglected children played mischievous pranks in their uncomfortable home. Poor man! like Mr. Jelleby, he prayed that none of his daughters might ever have a mission.

Go to Mrs. Biffles in your own character, as an honest white man or woman, and you will receive no favors at her hands. You must "take care of yourself." She will tell you "that is what every one should do in this world, and she has no time to pause in your behalf." No matter what your woes may be, you can draw no tears from Mrs. Biffles' eyes. But send her a negro, or represent yourself to have escaped from jail, and her arms and purse are at once opened. An escaped slave may firmly anticipate board, lodging, and the use of everything in her dwelling; the sympathizing tears of the fair lady, and a nice little sum of money to assist him in his travels, while the convict would be hidden in the cellar and sent upon his way rejoicing, with plenty of good advice, and a copy of Watts' Hymns in his pocket. In fact, to sum up all in a few words, Mrs. Biffles is like many other people. Public miseries and wrongs excite their deepest sympathy, while private sorrows are unheeded. The sufferings of those around them awaken no interest in their bosoms. Nay, they will even abuse their own servants, neglect those who have claims upon their kindness, and wound the feelings of others with whom they are associated, while they bemoan the woes of some oppressed race, sect or body, and even worship its unworthy members to an abject and servile degree.

As Mrs. Biffles pretends to be such a devout philanthropist, people very often send *white* objects of charity to her dwelling, and we could relate numerous instances of the way she receives them.

One day, a half starved, and ragged white boy, called at the door of Mrs. Biffles' dwelling, and asked for work. He had been sent there by some one. On the step, he was met by Mrs. Biffles' *adopted* favorite little African, and the following dialogue ensued :—

Starving White Boy—Does your master want a boy to work?

Little African—I ain't got no master, he's no 'count. I libs wid missus, and she doesn't hab *white* pussons 'bout.

Starving White Boy—But tell her I am very tired and hungry, and if she will give me a bit of bread, I'll be so thankful for it. Tell her I have no home.

Little African—No use to tell her dat. She wouldn't do nuffin for you, 'case you are not *colored* enough. Missus say she's not going to help vagabonds. White people can help demselves, *missus* says. Yes, missus says de Lord lubs his dark skinned children de best. So you'd better go away, white boy, for missus has got a berry cross bull dog in de yard.

That she feels for the negro, there is no doubt; but instead of being actuated by the impulses of a good heart, she is only lost in a monomaniacal zeal, which seems to effect many weak minded women, in whose families insanity has long been hereditary. Hundreds of destitute white widows have gone to Mrs. Biffles, with the most conclusive proofs of their *honesty*, and with deplorable evidences of their *want*, but she always sends them away with a religious tract, or the memoir of an escaped slave, or the confessions and reformation of a pardoned convict. She offers them neither food nor money. Mrs. Biffles' husband is wealthy, and she gives largely in aid of "colored emancipation," but has never contributed a penny to help her own race and sex, who are toiling and suffering in this great city.

There is another class of female philanthropists, who manage to get a living by sponging around among friends and acquaintances; and who are always disturbing the happiness of every body they meet, with the most violent declarations of what they *could* do, if they only had a *chance*. They never work, but are forever talking about the inadequacy of the compensation for female labor. They are great nuisances wherever you find them.

LIZZIE BLAIR.

LIZZIE BLAIR:

THE LITTLE HUNCHBACK.

Thou art *not* beautiful—yet thy young face
Makes up in sweetness what thee lacks in grace;
Thou art not beautiful—yet thy blue eyes
Steal o'er the soul like sunshine o'er the skies:—
And heaven, that gives to thee each mental grace,
Has stamp'd the angel on thy sweet young face.—MRS. WELBY.

LIZZIE Blair is a vest-maker,—a poor, forlorn little creature. Every Saturday evening she is seen hurrying down from the upper part of the city, bearing beneath her arm the bundle of work over which she has toiled during the past week. She is so bent and crooked, that it pains one's heart to look at her; but should you chance to speak to her, or even to look steadfastly into her pale face, her large mild eyes, and gentle smile, will make you murmur to yourself—

"Oh, how beautiful she might have been, but for that deformity!"

The little crossing sweeper looks hopefully into that pleasant countenance, as he holds out his chilly fingers ; and the blind beggar at the corner, knows the halting step, for it has paused beside him many a time, when there was one extra penny in the little old purse which might be given. Poverty has taught the little hunchback how the poor suffer, and her life-long misfortune has made her compassionate to others. When her work is paid for, and more taken for the ensuing week, she goes home quite happy that she has given satisfaction, and that to-morrow is a day of rest. She can then think and pray, for it is the Sabbath. She may then go to church, and take a quiet walk or read a favorite book, without neglecting the daily work, by which she earns her bread. The church pew opener does not pay much attention to the little hunchback. He puts her in a pew far from the pulpit, and destitute of cushions ; but she does not care far that, she can join in the prayer, and listen to the singing, and her soul's best feelings can float on the grand music of the old organ, far, far above this selfish world. Her mind can there dwell for awhile amidst the angels, forgetful of the misshapen body in which it makes its earthly habitation. Sometimes the sight of the people coming out of church, makes her sorrowful, for she sees so many of them have friends and relatives beside them. One lady hangs on her husband's arm, another has her daughter by the hand, and a brother and a sister, or a father and daughter, walk together so happily. The poor little cripple has no one to love her, and she wraps her shawl about her with a heavy sigh. No husband's arm will ever circle *her*, no babe will be enfolded to her bosom, and yet what a heart she has, and how devotedly she *could* have loved!

Listen. If you will never mention it aloud, we will tell you the secret of the poor little soul,—a secret *she* hides from all but her God, yet which has moistened her pillow with many a bitter tear.

The hunchback is in love. Every drop of her heart's blood, every impulse of her soul, is given to one man, whom she believes to be the perfection of human excellence and virtue, while he cares nothing for the little creature, to whom his smile or kindly glance is worth a kingdom.

Years ago, when the poor girl had a father's home to dwell in, this man strove to win her love, for the mere pleasure of the triumph, knowing all the while that he was doing wrong, and bringing sorrow to an innocent heart. *Now* her love is his, but time has taught her the folly of worldly dreams. And yet, despite his indifference, she would work her fingers to the bone to do him a service. She would lay down her life at any moment, to save him from harm. Sometimes they meet. Once in a long while she shakes hands with him, and goes home to ponder over the rare happiness, and console herself with the thought that they may meet in heaven, where her ugly form shall no longer hide her loving heart from him, and that he will there learn her silent truth and constancy.

Few guess the story of the hunchback's heart, but all who know her, feel sincere compassion. The old woman with whom she boards, has a kindly word of comfort and a smile for her now and then, and the children of the house flock around her for a kiss or a fairy tale. Her employers pay her wages with a friendly air, and even the people of the little shops, at which she spends her slender earnings, greet her with pleasant glances. All this is a balm to her soul, for which she thanks God each night before sleeping, and which lightens her daily toil.

When the stars shine down upon the world at night, they see no purer heart than hers. The morning sun never calls a laboring mortal to more patient industry. Days glide on, and bear the little cripple down the stream of time, to the sad music of her hidden love dream, while the neglectful throng, turning to gaze upon fair faces and graceful forms, forget or do not perceive the inner life which makes the hunchback beautiful in the sight of angels.

The sorrows of the poor little hunchback, are hardly any less than those of many of her sisters of the *needle*, who flock to the city and lodge in boarding house attics, and sew and sew by day and night, for barely enough to satisfy the demands of their landlady, who gives them a room six by ten, without lights or fire, and with scarcely a decent bed or chair, for three to four dollars a week. Oh, if women who live by the needle would only shun the city, and seek homes in the country, and in villages and towns where there is less competition and more hospitality, their destinies might be far happier. Think not that sorrow is only confined to cripples. Many and many a young girl with a comely form and a pretty face, is now sitting at work in her garret, and with a sad and heavy heart broods over unrequited love, and sighs for sympathy. Many a poor girl with homely features and shabby clothes, weeps herself to sleep at night, because the world slights her and people do not treat her kindly. Often and often a lonely woman feels her heart chooking her, as she hears the joyous laughter of those who have kind friends in plenty, and who are by fortune exempt from toil.

There is in every breast, a secret mystery, which the world may never know ; and in the breast of a lonely, toiling woman, that secret often corrodes and wastes her life away. It is sorrowful to contemplate the silent, untold workings of wretched, pent up hearts, which throb and beat with dull hope, until they wither beneath the weight of despair. New York is full of aching hearts, and we presume that the hearts of needle-women in particular, must go on aching until their throes of anguish terminate in death. But the time is fast approaching when the needle will be laid aside, and women who have been depending upon their *hands*, will turn to occupations which yield a better remuneration, and with which there are more encouraging associations.

OLIVE ROLAND.

MRS. OLIVE ROLAND.

THE DASHING WIDOW.

Coquet and coy at once her air,
Both studied, though both seem neglected:
Careless she is with artful care,
Affecting to seem unaffected.—*Congreve.*

MRS. Roland is a young and very handsome widow, who lives, Heaven knows how, in the greatest luxury, and moves in the first society. She is highly accomplished, and is an adept in all those little arts of fascination which can only be acquired by long and continued practice, and which often transform plain women into belles and beauties. Mrs. R. is tall, and moves with the majesty of an empress. Her hair is bewitching, and her long eye lashes sweep her cheeks when she looks downward; you would think her cold and stately at first sight, but when she chooses, she can be gentle and confiding as a dove. She has a bewildering way of smiling up into the eyes of her adorers, which quite defies description. She still wears her sable "weeds," and probably will do so until she espouses another husband, for she knows the effect of such a toilet upon her fair complexion, and on no account would she relinquish the advantage. Besides, it is a delicate way of announcing that she is in the matrimonial market. Young girls are very indignant when they see these charms working upon those who should be their admirers. They pronounce her forward, and say she is fond of flirting.

To Tompkins, she whispers that she only endures the attentions of Brown, (poor fellow,) out of pity. To Brown, she confides the fact that she cannot endure Tompkins, but that her foolish, good-natured little heart, will not allow her to hurt his feelings by avoiding him. To Wilson she murmurs, "Oh, I do *so* love to waltz with *you*, you keep *such* time." And in half an hour, she promises Brown her hand for the next dance, with the remark—"Certainly, if only to avoid standing up again with that awkward fellow, Wilson."

No one has ever breathed a word against Mrs. Roland's character. There are no whispers afloat which tell of awakened suspicion, and yet, she is living sumptuously without any apparent means, and, stranger still, no duns assail her door, and no unpaid tradesmen speak complainingly of their little bills. Did Mr. Roland leave money behind him? No one ever heard of it, if he did.

Last summer Mrs. Roland was at Newport, at Saratoga, and at Lake George. She had troops of friends and admirers. Indeed she is never without an attendant cavalier, and some obsequious swain is always ready to obey her every wish. Though, it is singular that nobody knows anything of the lady's past life. Ask them who she is, and they will reply, "Oh! a handsome young widow, from New York; we were introduced to her by the Browns." The Browns in their turn, know nothing of the lady's birth-place or family, or the standing or profession of her deceased spouse. Enquire their opinion on any of these matters and they will answer: "Oh, why, she is *rich*, and no one would like to appear suspicious enough to ask her. Every one *must* see that she is charming and aristocratic, and everybody knows her!"

This is true enough. Mrs. Roland never lets an eligible acquaintance slip. No person who is worth knowing escapes her, and, best of all, they make the first apparent advances, and she is sought instead of seeking. None ever say that "Mrs. Roland called on me," it is always "I called on Mrs. Roland." The secret springs of her manœuvers are unseen by the very parties who are the most interested.

To her *dear* friends, Mrs. Roland is in the habit of relating her experiences. She has been in England, France and Italy, dined with German Barons, and vowed eternal friendship to many a Spanish Donna. She has waltzed with an Earl, received a proposition of marriage from a Count, and refused five Lords in one season at London. She also danced with the Prince of Wales at the ball given in his honor in New York. Her dashing friend, Captain Baltic, was killed in the Crimea, and sent his love to her with his last breath, and she witnessed half the Mexican war with her own eyes, and was the first to grasp the hand of brave old Taylor, after his victory at Monterey. She deeply sympathised with poor, brave, handsome, Santa Anna. How *one* young woman, not yet eight and twenty, could have passed through such scenes, and traversed so many lands, is a perfect mystery. But Mrs. Roland always manages to tell these anecdotes without mentioning the circumstances under which she encountered them, or the names or relations of her traveling companions ; she gives only a general idea of sumptuousness and universal homage, which makes you almost afraid to ask another question lest you should discover that you are addressing a princess in disguise. To a lady, Mrs. Roland is just as fascinating as she is to a gentleman. She will run to meet you, seize you by both hands, and imprint a kiss upon your cheek, ejaculating, "Oh, I'm so delighted that you have come," and insist upon your having "just a little lunch." Then she will take you up into her boudoir, produce her perfumes to refresh you after your walk, admire your new bonnet, and lay it aside with the words, "But then, *everything* you wear is so charming; you have such exquisite taste and know just what becomes you." She will delicately tease you about the very suitor you like most to be teased about, and then sigh and say, "Ah! how miserable one feels to be alone and unprotected." This will naturally lead you to speak on the subject of her admirers, and she will confess that one has proposed and been refused, and that another has threatened to kill himself. She tells all in such a modest way, not in the boasting style a girl always adopts, but as if she did not mean to divulge a word, until you drew it out of her.

Be you man or woman, you will inevitably be fascinated by Mrs. Roland, and when you hear of her espousal to some rich husband, you will say, "he is a lucky man, and has secured a treasure." But under no circumstances will you ever know more of her real history than you do now, for the *dashing widow* is, and always will be, a charming but impenetrable mystery.

It should be borne in mind though, that *dashing* young widows have a cruel and malicious habit of casting reflections upon all pretty women who endeavor to maintain themselves by bodily or mental exertion at some honest occupation.

Young Dobbs says that Miss Harriet the music teacher, is such an interesting girl, and really, very pretty.

" Oh, dear, but she is horribly *low*," sneers the dashing widow. " Why, she has worn the same dress every day for three months."

" Well, she is only a poor girl," responds Dobbs, who by the way, is half human, and not afraid to show it. " She has a mother and two little nieces to support."

" Pshaw, that's the old story. I never yet knew one of those creatures who *hadn't* some such an excuse. Why, you don't suppose that she supports all that family with what she gets for music lessons, do you ?"

" I certainly do," ejaculates Dobbs, opening his eyes, " How else could she ?"

The dashing widow executes one of her bewitching postures and laughs merrily. Then she archly says : " Why, Mr. Dobbs, how *very* innocent you are !"

LAURA ELMER.

LAURA ELMER:

THE SORROWING MOTHER.

Alone she sate—alone!—that worn-out word,
So idly spoken and so coldly heard;
Yet all that poets sing, and grief hath known,
Of hope laid waste, knells in that word—*alone!*—New Timon.

THERE are spots in the great city, always teeming with misery and degradation, where, on every side, the heart is sickened by the sight of faces with deeply graven wrinkles, that show vice and intemperance;—spots where children who, in happy homes, might be types of purity and beauty, are loathsome, scowling objects, already old in crime, and where women lost to modesty, and neglectful of person and attire, seem even more degraded than the beastly men around them. Among these creatures the eye may sometimes fall upon a face which seems more marked by sorrow than by crime, which, pinched and wan, and sallow, excites pity rather than repugnance, and makes the beholder wonder what series of misfortunes placed it among such scenes. Sometimes the face is a man's, oftener it is a woman's. Such a countenance is that of Laura Elmer. Her portrait is before you.

There she sits. The great tears are pouring down her cheeks, and falling upon the crumpled edges of the old hood, thrown carelessly over her tangled hair. Her past is full of woe, her present of remorse, and grim starvation crouches in the shadows of the hopeless future. A bitter lot is hers; and strange and terrible the thought, that the sorrows of all her useless life were poured upon her head by the hand of an indulgent mother, and a kind though foolish father.

Years and years ago, a young couple married, and emigrated from the eastern states to a wild and newly settled region of the west. They strove diligently, and in the course of years grew prosperous and respected. The log cabin was exchanged for a frame house, that in turn gave place to a stone mansion, and, but for one circumstance, they would have been happy. This bitter drop in their cup of life, was the early death of their children. One after one their babes were laid in the grave, and they looked forward sorrowfully to an old age unblest by the filial affection of son or daughter. At last another babe was sent to them. It was a little girl, beautiful as a rosebud, and with every promise of health in her dimpled cheeks, and rounded limbs. They named her Laura, and she grew in strength and beauty.

Like too many American women, the loving mother fancied idleness to be essential to delicacy,—that a *lady* should not labor. And when in her own homespun way, she declared that "her Laura should never bring the water to wash her own hands," she believed that she was doing the best she could for her child, in thus dooming her to a life of helplessness and inaction.

Spoiled and petted, Laura grew into girlhood, utterly ignorant of every domestic duty. The mother still churned, and baked, and ironed; but she excluded her daughter from participation in any thing which might soil her fingers. The snowy home-bleached linen was still made into garments, under the roof of the old homestead, but Laura never drew a needle through seam or gather. Those womanly arts which make home attractive and comfortable, were too coarse and commonplace for her attention. She could thrum a few airs on the guitar, do a little in bead work, and embroider green parots and red shepherds in Berlin wool, and that was all. Her days were spent lolling in the parlor and perusing trashy yellow covered literature, and her cheeks were constantly bedewed by imbecile tears, shed for the fictitious woes of some imaginary hero or maiden. The extent of her exertions was the attiring of her own person for a visit to exhibit a new bonnet, or a weak interchange of small talk with some confidential friend. Her deluded parents witnessed this waste of life and intellect, with the utmost satisfaction. Their efforts and self-denial were crowned with success. They believed that Laura had grown to be "a perfect lady."

Pretty, and the heiress of all her father's possessions, Laura had many suitors. One of them was a young man from the city. On him she bestowed her hand. She thought she also gave him her heart. Loving her fondly, the young husband was blind to all her faults. He considered her a model of perfection. In compliance with her wishes, he removed at once to the city, where her character began to shine forth in its true colors. The smouldering evil imbibed by novel reading, now burst into flame. She became reckless and wild. At last the frightened husband ventured to remonstrate, but he was met with a flood of tears, and fits of hysterics, such as only women of Laura's rearing can perform so well. Again, and again, the scene was enacted, and soon quarrels were of every day occurrence. The house, always upside down, was the picture of discomfort. The servants, who knew that the mistress was a perfect nonentity, wasted their time, and plundered the pantry to their heart's content. Scores of "cousins" were entertained by Biddy and Maggie, while their master's meat and puddings were either done to a crisp, or put upon the table raw. The plates, knives, and forks, were specimens of what neglect could do to steel and china. Met only by disorder and ill temper at home, her husband soon sought happiness elsewhere. There were other houses, other places to dine, and other and pleasanter women. The neglect which she had brought upon herself, was soon a frightful source of complaint, and the pair seemed to vie with each other in extravagance and dissipation. At last there came a crash! Ruin stared them in the face, and the poor old parents sold out their farm and homestead, and came at once to the succor of their idolized child. Vain efforts! The path was too far trodden. A little while longer, and then the mask fell forever.

Ruined, broken-hearted, and dishonored,

Laura's husband sought release in death. One morning the servants found their wretched master lying upon the floor a corpse!

About this time, Laura's good old parents also died, and she was left alone with three children, as useless and worthless as herself. Creditors seized what she had, and compelled by the prospect of starvation, she endeavored to earn her daily bread. But all that she could do was coarse sewing. Receiving this "slop work," and placing out her sons as errand boys in stores, she thus eked out a miserable existence of destitution. Even now industry and effort might have done something. Had the poor home been tidy, the scanty food properly prepared for them, the boys would have sought it as an ark of refuge, and at their own fireside they might have grown to be the props of her old age, and become virtuous and respected men. But the thought of such attention to her home never entered Laura's mind. Her leisure moments were spent in bewailing her lost luxury, and in solacing her woe with the contents of a little black bottle, which replaced the champagne and catawba to which she had been accustomed. Dirt and squalor were on every hand. The boys were left to themselves, and rated for ingratitude with maudlin tears, and they went rapidly into dissipation. Step by step they sunk, until a loathsome tenement house was the only shelter for the head once pillowed upon down, and guarded by wealth from the very winds of heaven.

This woe-begone, wrinkled woman, and her children—where are they? The eldest son is a drunkard, the youngest is a convicted felon, and the daughter is an outcast, leading an infamous life.

Dependent upon the fitful generosity of her sottish son and outcast daughter, or upon the charity of strangers, the wretched Laura treads the road which leads toward the hospital or almshouse, a living warning to all who encourage their daughters in idleness and educate them to believe that a woman's brains and hands were made for nothing.

On a pleasant afternoon, Laura may be seen sitting on the steps of the tenement house where she lives; and when the black bottle has done its work, she will loudly bewail the ingratitude of her children to a mother who has done so much for them, ending always with the boast—

"I never brought the water to wash my own hands, when I was young. I was brought up a lady!"

Ah, there are many sorrowing mothers,

weeping over children whom they have petted, spoiled, and ruined. It is a too common notion that sons and daughters should be reared in idleness, if they expect to be "any body" in the world. 'Tis a pity, though, that such folly prevails among those whose limited means are insufficient for perpetual extravagance. If the rich were the only people who raise their children thus, it would not be so bad; but when almost every poor mother we see, is straining her utmost, and depriving herself of nearly all the comforts of life, for the sake of educating her daughters in tastes and feelings away beyond their actual position, we deem it our duty, as a woman, and authoress, to point out the evil. If mothers would reflect—if they *could* but behold the thousands of dissipated and vice-branded females now writhing in the mental and bodily tortures of a criminal existence, and trace back their histories to the cradle, they would shudder to learn the cause of their going down to shame. All women are but creatures of circumstances, and easily made miserable or happy by teachings in childhood. Mothers who *love* their children, should study the subject, and not let their *false* pride deter them from performing their duty.

SIGNORINA ADELINA.

SIGNORENA ADELINA.

THE OPERA SINGER.

Why did she love him? Curious fool be still,—
Is human love the growth of human will?—BYRON.

USH! Do you hear that thrilling voice? What a beautiful creature! Dark lustrous eyes, such as Italian alone can boast of. A pure skin, with a glow like that of the sunset upon her cheeks, and lips which seemed to challenge soft caresses. No wonder the applause shakes the theatre to its centre. Bravo! little beauty, we could listen forever.

There she stands bending her graceful head in smiling thanks. The footlights fall upon her robe of snowy satin, and make the jewels upon her bosom gleam and glitter. By her beauty she might be a queen, but she is only the child of humble Italian parents, just a little higher born than the Lazzaroni.

An American musician went to Italy, hoping amid soft airs to win the hue of health back to his pale cheek, and to drive away the incipient symptoms of consumption, which, his physician told him, threatened ere long to waste away his life, and tear him from the enjoyment of his well earned fame, and the love of friends who had gathered around him. He daily spent many hours among some grey old ruins, which teemed with wild legends and poetical associations. There was a fountain there in the ruins, and hither a beautiful child came at noon to fill her earthen pitcher, and lave her dainty hands and feet. Her garb was coarse, and betokened mean origin. But once, as she lingered in the shadow of the crumbling walls, she sung a song, so sweetly and with such expression, that the invalid was charmed and astonished. Speaking to the child, he praised her voice, and asked her to sing again. Often, after that, she came to the grey ruins, and always at the stranger's bidding, went through her little stock of ballads. His praises pleased her, and she felt, rather than knew, that she was appreciated as well as admired.

At last, when returning health permitted the musician to seek his native clime, he went to the child's parents and said to them—

"Your daughter has a magnificent voice.

With proper education she will make a Prima Donna. May I take her with me?"

The mother and father were needy and avaricious, and they grasped the gold he offered them.

"Yes, Signor," they answered, "and may God bless you."

Years were spent in hard study and practice, and with music, the fair girl acquired also the mien of a refined lady. The little foreign accent still audible in her speech, was only an additional charm, and a great success was prophecied for her debut.

The night came. Arrayed in her white robes, with a glittering jewel upon her raven tresses, Adelina stepped forth upon the stage, and even before her voice had charmed them, every eye beamed her a welcome. When the performances closed, the applause was so heartfelt and universal, that she sobbed for very joy.

Following her triumph, came many others. Her beauty proved as attractive as her voice. *Billetdoux*, anonymous presents, love verses on scented paper, and magnificent boquets of hot-house flowers, were showered upon her, and some bolder than the rest, had already uttered their praises in her presence. Among them was a young man named Edward Blair, and who seemed, to poor Adelina's eyes, all that is admirable in man. He told her that she was beautiful, and she blushed with pleasure. He whispered that life passed in her society would be a Heaven upon earth, and she longed to tell him, that she lived only when he was near her. By and bye, she sung only to him. When the house was full, and all eyes were riveted on the young singer's face, she looked for him amidst the crowd, and finding him, cared only for his applause and his bright smile of approbation.

Dreams of quiet home life hovered around her pillow, and she thought sweetly of being his wife, and sharing the joys and sorrows of his existence, and this might some day come to pass, she hoped, for she knew well that he loved her. But does the spider love the fly he seeks to entrap within its net? Does the worm that eats the sweetness from the white rose's heart, love the rich flower it ruins? Alas! it is natural for woman to believe and man to deceive.

One sweet warm day in June, when the soft air was full of fragrant odors, and the sky was blue and cloudless, Edward Blair asked Adelina to ride with him. They went away from the noise of the city, and sought a broad smooth road which winds out into the country. The beautiful singer was very happy, and her escort seemed that day in more than usual spirits.

The light wheeled vehicle bore them along, until turning down a green and shady lane, they looked upon the silvery Hudson. Here they paused, and Edward Blair's arm twined about Adelina's slender waist. He breathed hot passionate love words in her ear, and sought with pleading glances for a sweet return. For a moment she basked in the bright dream of happiness, for an instant she lay folded to his bosom; but suddenly she started from him, with aversion. She saw through the words he uttered, and then knew that he wooed her not for his wife. For the first time, she was conscious of the dangerous position in which her public life inevitably placed her, and the bitterest thought of all was that insult should come from one in whose manly honor she had so trustfully confided. In her agony she prayed to die.

"Drive me home," she said, when she could master her voice, "Drive me home. We must never meet again."

And they never have met again. Edward Blair has long repented of the insult he proffered her, and with increased esteem he has conceived a stronger love. He would woo her honorably, *now*, he would beg her pardon upon his bended knees, but never while she lives, will poor Adelina touch, even with the hem of her flowing robe, the man who broke her girlhood's dream of innocence and love.

Her voice is still as charming and her face as beautiful as ever, but her heart within is cold as marble. She will never marry. Love's taper burns only once within a woman's breast, and her's has been extinguished by the rushing torrent of man's selfish passion.

There are numerous Edward Blairs who amuse themselves with frequenting the opera, not so much to enjoy the music as to admire and become acquinted with the young women whose pretty faces and voluptuous forms secure them places on the stage. Yet it is not always that these connoiseurs of female beauty meet with an Adelina. Like women in private life, Opera Singers, whether Prima Donnas or of the Corps de Ballet, they require clothing, fire, food and shelter, and have also a thousand other wants and necessities peculiar to their associations and profession, which slender salaries cannot provide for. They look for all advancement to come through the same channel—the public—the *people*—and hence they risk more and venture farther out into the perils of the world, than wives and daughters whose positions do not call them beyond domestic seclusion.

BIDDY McKAY.

MRS. BIDDY M[c]KAY:

THE VAGRANT.

Ah, whisky, whisky! bane of life,
Spring of tumult, source of strife;
Could we but half thy curses tell,
The wise would wish thee safe in hell

BIDDY McKay began life in the city of New York, under the name of O'Rooney, which was written on a placard pinned to her dingy garments, on the morning when she was found in a basket suspended from the knob of a door. She was conveyed at once to the poor house, and brought up on the frugal diet allowed at such establishments, until she reached the age of thirteen, when she was "bound out" to a judicious matron, who thought such a proceeding the cheapest way of obtaining "help." Biddy came out of the establishment, with a very shortly cropped head of coarse black hair, and a long tow apron which covered her from the shoulders to her ankles, and was immediately set to cleaning knives, scouring pans, scrubbing, washing and ironing. On Monday she had her ears boxed for the purpose of making her "smart" during the week, and on Saturday they were boxed again to make her still smarter. She had even less than the poor house allowance for supper, and was expected to put up with the eternal abuse of her employer's children, who called her names, pinched her black and blue, and threw chewed bread and butter in her face, without the least compunction, and by sheer hunger, was driven into her first dishonesty. She took to purloining cakes from a cupboard, in which dainties, such as she was never allowed to taste, were kept by her mistress. For this act, poor Biddy received a severe whipping, but the stolen food was very tempting, and she repeated the offence without discovery. Coming of age emancipated Biddy from the thraldom of her first mistress, and she departed quite an adept in deceit and treachery.

The next three years of Biddy's life were passed in changing from one "place" to another, and experience with many mistresses caused her to become still more subtle and treacherous every day of her existence. Her's was the boldest face presented at the intelligence office, and none of her compeers were more dexterous at petty larceny in every kitchen. She stuffed sheets into the rag-bag, poured pounds of butter into the "soap fat," and entertained her admirers on the choicest tit-bits from the family table, laid all the miraculous disappearances of cold mutton and turkey's legs to "the cat," wore her mistresses bonnets and shawls on state occasions, and listened at key holes for the family secrets, which she circulated throughout the neighborhood. At last she wound up her single life, by bestowing her hand upon Dennis McKay, who kept a small but thriving corner grocery.

She and Dennis began life in Hibernian style, by "treating" all their friends and companions to whisky. Their merry making lasted several months, and Biddy grew very fond of the stimulants. Waiting behind the bar, as she often did, gave her an opportunity to indulge as frequently as she felt inclined, and by the time the first young McKay was ushered into the world, both father and mother were in the habit of getting drunk as often as they felt like it. Quarrels had become frequent, and bottles flew about the dwelling, smashing windows and knocking heads, and frequently rendering the doctor's attendance necessary. During the presidential election,

Dennis got into a row, put out several eyes, smashed half a dozen heads, and broke two or three noses, and was finally carried home upon a shutter by his comrades, with several fractured bones and no discernible features to his countenance. Dennis soon after died, and Biddy, who had done nothing but quarrel with him for many years, now cried. Her shrieks were heard all over the neighborhood, while the friends made preparations for an "illigant wake," and have a night of it. There was an immense funeral, and poor Dennis was buried.

Three months afterward, Biddy married the shop man, a youth of two and twenty, and took him as a partner in the store. The shop man had a brother, a stout, red haired individual, fond of smoking short black pipes, and always redolent of onions. This relative became an inmate of the family, and stood in high favor with Biddy, a fact which gave his brother unlimited dissatisfaction, until one morning they eloped with each other, taking with them all the cash. The husband could have borne the loss of his blooming wife, but the cash was too much to part with quietly, and the treacherous brother was pursued and arrested for the robbery. The property was found upon his person, and he was sent into captivity for six years. The faithless spouse, meanwhile, falling into an argument with another interesting specimen of the fair sex, lost command of her temper, and bit, scratched, and otherwise maltreated her opponent in such a manner that she was also consigned to durance vile.

Emerging from her retirement, at the termination of her sentence, Biddy commenced a regular persecution of her husband, contriving by abuse or wheedling, to obtain a sufficient supply of money to enable her to live without labor and sink into dissipation.

Wherever the worst and most degraded drunkards are gathered together, you may find Biddy's bruised face and long figure She has been arrested more than once for theft, and often gets to fighting in the streets. She staggers about, with her black bottle peeping from beneath her tattered shawl, and makes decency shudder at the thought that such a creature bears the name of woman. Vice seems born in many breasts, and it may be that Biddy would have been the same, even with the best education. Yet, we almost believe that the hard, unkindly treatment of the bound girl, may have influenced the woman's life.

Dear reader, did you ever think *what* it *is* to be an orphan, with the alms house for your home, until you are "bound out" to a mistress whose soul and purse prefers "taken girls" to full grown women, who eat hearty, and expect their wages at the end of the month? You *never* thought of it! Well, if you *would* think it over, seriously, perhaps you might see a very gloomy picture of what some desolate hearts endure. We believe that many a bad woman was made so by the treatment she received at the hands of her mistress when a child. It is during our childhood that we imbibe the spirit of good or evil, which is ever after uppermost in our dispositions, to be developed according to the circumstances controlling our destinies. Much has been written to prove the *innate* depravity of this or that particular person, no matter how piously reared and instructed; but, as a general rule, if two children, exactly similar in every peculiarity of mind and body, were separated at birth, and placed in directly opposite situations, and under opposite treatment, we may depend upon their maturing to a striking dissimilarity. One will be *good*, the other will be *bad*. We admit that after events must have considerable influence, but if their characters are *fully tested*, there can be only *one* result.

RHODA ALWYN.

RHODA ALWYN.

THE PERJURED BRIDE.

Dumb *jewels* often, in their silent kind,
More than quick words, do move a woman's mind.
SHAKSPEARE.

Get place and wealth if posssible, with grace,
If not, by *any* means get wealth and place.—POPE.

RHODA Alwyn is young, beautiful, and accomplished, and moves in the best society. Her mother, a handsome widow, and a belle and beauty, has spared no pains on her education, but has finished her daughter, after the most improved pattern, at Madame B's. seminary. Rhoda can dance, sing and play, and is able to sustain a brilliant flirtation throughout a whole season, or to glide through the mazes of the dance from midnight until morning, without the least fatigue, and above all is acknowledged to be the best dressed young lady found anywhere. Mrs. Alwyn has cultivated her charms and accomplishments as she would have improved any other valuable piece of property. The more perfect Rhoda's beauty, the greater her matrimonial market value, and for this auction she has been reared and educated. When Turkish parents sell their children, we roll up our eyes in horror, and groan over their depravity, but we look smilingly on and fold our hands approvingly, while Mrs. B. consigns her young daughter to the highest purchaser, and gives an old libertine a husband's right over a pure and innocent maiden. We, who are Christians, and kneel in our cushioned pews three times every Sunday—*we* do this. Rhoda has a heart—a soft, warm heart it would have been, *we think*, with proper care and nursing, but society and mamma do not approve of hearts, and there is nothing so foolish as natural tender feelings.

"A well educated girl," says Mrs. Alwyn, "as she fans herself upon the sofa," always thinks first of a settlement. Love in a cottage is a low absurdity. In high society, *respect* is all that is requisite to feel towards a husband. Look at the French ; they are models, I'm sure ; and *they* always marry judiciously, at least among the upper classes. So, Rhoda, for mercy's sake, don't let *your* affections become entangled with anything below twenty thousand a year."

And the young girl, acquiescing in the wisdom of her mother's opinion, wonders that she is not quite happy, and thinks sometimes of what she might have been had *somebody* been as rich as he was handsome. Rhoda has been "*out*" four seasons, and is now twenty years old. Mamma has told her that she must make her choice this year, if possible; for a marriageable daughter is a great drain upon any income, and American beauty soon fades when it is out of its teens. The girl knows that she must give up her freedom in a very little while. She will have her carriage, fine establishment and diamonds. Hundreds, fair and young as she, will envy her. But that old man, how *can* she ever call him husband? and the wicked thought steals through her heart that he *is* very old, and that if he should die leaving her a wealthy widow, it would be no harm then to let Charles Graham woo and win her. In the darkness of her chamber, at the dead hour of midnight, her cheek grows crimson as she looks upon her guilty heart. Does her mamma know this? Does she ever falter or repent, fearing lest that fiery furnace, over which the young soul is hanging, should destroy its purity? Does she ever remember, as she draws back her rustling robes, lest they should brush against some poor lost creature, who passes her upon the crowded pave, that a woman who marries for money is no better than one of those. Alas! no. The glitter of diamonds has blinded and the chink of gold deafened her. That old man is a sinner, but he is an excellent match. He has vices, but then he has money also, and bless you, *that* is everything. And mamma fans herself and speaks to other mammas of "Rhoda's excellent prospects." Then the old ladies play a little game to blind each other and themselves, and speak of "good settled principles," and "old men's darlings," and the "inconsistency of wild boys," and mention the price of their daughter's hands and hearts in delicate terms, such as, "Ah, well! Flora has eighty thousand settled on herself," and "Kate's dear good old husband is worth half a million."

Yes, Rhoda will probably be married this year; Grace Church will witness her nuptials, and the Fifth Avenue will smile upon them, and even while she bends her graceful head, and vows to love, honor and obey, her heart will be far, far away in another, happier scene, and the face of Charles Graham will rise before her, with the look upon it which he wore when last they met. It was not wise of Mrs. Alwyn to let her daughter spend those bright months *unchaparoned* at B——, for it was there she met that face of which she thinks so often, and heard that voice whose echo will haunt her soul forever. They were together on the beach, on the breezy hill side, and in the pleasant farm-house parlor. They read each other's hearts and they might have loved purely, had she been a poor country girl. When they parted, it was with the hope of meeting soon again, and of some day being even yet dearer and nearer to each other. Charles treasured Rhoda's image, and was happier than tongue can tell. But she was in the vortex of fashion, amid the whirl of city life. Then the warning voice of mamma and the cold snear of society! Could she marry a poor man? Could *she* live in a cottage, and do without rich garments and servants? Her heart failed her; she was a belle, a beauty and a stylish woman, and not fitted for a plain man's wife. Mamma first scolded and then commanded. She inquired of Rhoda how she would like to feed the pigs, and have rag carpet on her parlor, and wondered what people would say when they heard of it. And when she had brought her daughter to a proper mood, dictated a cold, contemptuous refusal, and placing pen and paper before her, bade her write. The note was sent, but with it went unseen, a hasty scrawl, penned by a trembling hand, in which Rhoda bade a last farewell to her lover, and prayed that he might be happy and forget her.

That night, as Charles Graham walked to and fro, with burning cheek and dilating eye, twisting the little billet ruthlessly between his fingers, she who had written the words which pained him so, glided gaily through the dance, while those who gazed upon her noticed how pale and yet how beautiful she was. She thought they had parted forever then, and mamma fanned herself constantly and commended her own prudence. But as the weeks glided by, Rhoda hid little billets in her bosom, and, at last, even met her discarded lover clandestinely, although both were aware that an insurmountable barrier would soon arise between them. No one knew of these meetings, save a French waiting-maid, and there was no harm, only a little folly in them. No harm? But the black browed French woman winks and shrugs her shoulders and thinks how firmly she can establish herself in a situation when she holds the key of her mistress's secrets, as well as those of her wardrobe and bureau, and how when the nuptials are once over, their meetings might cause a separation and great scandal, were they discovered; and how Madame will not dare offend the maid who could bring her to such disgrace. And so Rhoda walks, tottering on the margin of a fearful gulf, led on by the beckoning fingers of love and ambition. She will not sacrifice all that splendor and share poverty with Charles Graham, and yet she cannot forbear the pleasure of seeing him, and hearing his love. She could not so far fly away from her mother's yoke, as to refuse the old man chosen for her, but she can disobey her at heart and run the risk of a discovery. The wedding morning is near at hand, the robe is fashioned, the white veil lies ready for the bride, and there is no warning in the air and no omen in the sky. No voice says to the old man, pause and consider! No angel bids the mother arise and save her daughter. Only conscience flushes Rhoda Alwyn's cheek, and causes her to tremble when the French maid's black eyes meet her own, and all is going on quietly and smoothly toward the end.

When the wedding is over and the stately mansion receives its guests, Charles Graham can visit its mistress when he chooses. The French woman will recognise him, and will shrug her shoulders many times, but the old bridegroom never saw them and can never guess of those fond kisses and loving words which she remembers. Like the calm before a storm, peace will dwell in their abode, even while the clouds of shame are creeping darkly around the sky. But when the tempest bursts, its shock will be all the more fearful. Beware, old man! Beware, manœuvring woman! Beware!

frail girl, tempted on every side, lest in that storm all hope on earth or in heaven be swept away forever.

Marrying for money is *fashionable* in New York, and perhaps two-thirds of the young women in the upper circles, are *sold* by their parents to the highest bidders. But a young girl with bright eyes and a gushing heart cannot mate with a dry old man. She may give him a husband's rights, but her love she can *not* barter in the same way. Love will seek out sympathy, and how many good, honest and pure hearts are at this moment being tempted to accept a rich husband and retain an idolized lover. Oh! parents, it is a *crime* to thus traffic in your children's flesh and teach them the road to perdition.

PRISCILLA WIGGINS.

PRISCILLA WIGGINS:

THE MAN HATER.

Oh! I am sick of this dark world,
My heart, my best affections blighted,
My sails of joy for ever furl'd,
My dawning hopes so soon benighted.—McIlvane.

ISS Priscilla Wiggins is a "strong minded" woman. She is sharp featured, high shouldered, gaunt and graceless. Her age can only be guessed at, for every secret on that subject has been carefully obliterated from the family Bible, and she is, at present, the head of a flourishing boarding school for young ladies, where morals are inculcated with the grammar, and where no male visitors are allowed to intrude. Her Circulars set forth these facts:—"The instructress is herself a devotee of science, who will endeavor to bend the minds of her young friends in the same direction; and that every young lady is expected to bring a knife and fork, a napkin ring, and a copy of Watts' Hymns; and furthermore, that no young gentlemen, even though they be brothers or cousins, can be permitted to call upon the pupils, as the strictest propriety and decorum will be observed throughout the establishment."

Every morning, after prayers, the young ladies of Miss Wiggins' establishment are assembled to hear the "Guide to Young Ladies," read aloud, and to study a chapter of the "Code of Etiquette," and, once a week, they are permitted to walk two by two, at the genteel snail's pace adopted by such institutions, when out for an airing. All the scholars are very pale and thin, and have little or no appetites. They would not laugh or run for all the world, and consider merriment the height of vulgarity. Many of them wear blue glasses, and the taste of the school leans decidedly towards corkscrew ringlets. As for Miss Wiggins, no "ology" escapes her, and the moment an "ism" emerges upon the field, she is quickly after it. She is very talkative, and if once allowed to secure your attention, she will keep you listening for hours, overwhelming you with arguments and stating "her views," in a manner which would astonish Lucy Stone. Miss Wiggins' pet theme, is the depravity of man, and his assumption of superiority over woman.

"Men are all alike," she observes. "Tyrants, every one of them. Thank fortune! I never allowed myself to be taken in the nets they spread. I never married; no indeed! I enjoyed my freedom too well. And I only wish all young women would be induced to follow my example; but, dear me, not one out of fifty, has resolution enough to keep her freedom." When Miss Wiggins says this, she shakes her corkscrew curls, and sighs aloud.

Whether Miss Wiggins is really a pattern for her sex, as she asserts, or whether the grapes are only sour, can best be judged by a short review of her past life and experience.

Priscilla Wiggins was born in Slab-town, in the winter of a long departed year. Her mother was a long, hard-featured country woman, and her father, a genuine Quaker, taught the youth of Slab-town their a b c's, and made them mind their p's and q's. The girl inherited no beauty from her parents, and possessed no charms peculiar to herself. Nevertheless, a greater stock of vanity never filled a feminine brain. As she grew up, her days were spent in the manufacture of new finery, the nights in dreams of conquests; and every masculine eye which rested upon her features, she supposed to be fascinated by her beauty. At seventeen she made her first decided effort at securing a captive. Jonathan Briggs was the largest, stupidest, and richest boy in her father's school. The other farmer's sons came only in the winter to pursue their education, but Jonathan, being exceedingly dull, was sent the whole year round, and sat among the girls and small children, stammering through his pages of reading lessons, and toiling over his multiplication " sums," when he was fast verging upon nineteen summers. Around this youth the fair Priscilla threw her most potent spells. She " told him his lesson," did his sums for him, gave notice of her father's approach during the performance of sundry prohibited pranks, and smiled upon him sweetly in school and out of school. In payment for these favors, she demanded Jonathan's undivided attention and homage, at all hours, and upon every occasion. At church, there was Priscilla waiting to be seen home by Jonathan. At singing school, there she was fastened upon his arm ; and at any social gathering, Priscilla Wiggins and Jonathan Briggs were paired off as a matter of course. Bye and bye the boy began to tire of this state of things. Though a lout, he was fond of pretty faces, and Priscilla's was anything but bewitching, yet there it was at his elbow on every occasion. Jonathan, like many other donkies, began to be restive. First of all, he tried to treat Priscilla coldly, but the fair damsel never noticed the change in his demeanor. Then he huffed her, but she clung to him all the closer. Next, poor Jonathan endeavored to avoid her, but she was not to be avoided, and finally the persecuted youth fairly ran away. It was at an "apple paring." All the peels were off, all the supper was eaten, and all the guests were departing, and Jonathan stood at the door, eyeing the pretty Betsey Bouncer, with a hopeful look, when Priscilla, in her usual way, approached and took his arm. Flesh and blood could not stand it. Jonathan turned around and said—

"I think you'd orter be 'shamed of yourself, I do!"

"Why, what's the matter, Johnny?" inquired Priscilla.

"I say you'd orter be 'shamed of yourself, a ketchin hold of me before I ask you!" said the youth. "You'r always a doing of it, you are. It's all very well to wait on you home once in a while, but I ain't 'goin to do it every single night. I ain't a courtin of you, and don't mean to neither. If your father is a teacher, why don't he teach you how to behave? I can't go any where without you go, and I can't come any where without you come, and I don't mean to stand it no longer. I'm 'goin to see hum who I like after this, and you needn't try to hinder me.—There now!" So saying, the exasperated Jonathan wrenched himself from Priscilla's grasp, and emancipated himself forever.

Priscilla was mortified, but not discouraged. There were other rich men's sons worth catching, and she persevered by laying her nets in the boldest and most decisive style, and without the least concealment of purpose. In ten years, there was not a single man in Slab-town in whose arms she had not fainted, or whose hand she had not lightly squeezed, and yet, at the mature age of twenty-seven, Miss Wiggins still retained her maiden name. By and by a handsome bachelor of fifty was called to the vacant pulpit of the Slab-town meeting house. He was peculiarly dignified and serious, and was understood to have remained unmarried, on account of the frivolity and light mindedness of women kind. He had remarked, at a tea party given in his honor, that he grieved to find so few of the sex who devoted themselves to the higher branches of literature and science, and immediately a great change began to be observable in Miss Priscilla. First she began to comb the hair off her forehead, and then she adopted glasses. Next she began to write poetry for the village paper, and finally she occupied the front seat in the middle isle of the meeting-house three times every Sabbath, rain or shine. In a short time, some intricate doctrinal point weighed so heavily upon her mind, that she was obliged to call upon her pastor, in order to satisfy herself of the truth of her misgivings, and having once received instructions, she went again and again to drink at the fountain of knowledge. The minister was pleased and flattered by this deference to his opinions. He loaned the anxious lady works on theology, the interesting passages marked with lead pencil. Slab-town wondered with all its might. Could it be that Miss Wiggins had really made a conquest? She herself was certain of it, and only waited for his proposition. One Thursday evening, Miss Wiggins and the minister were alone in the parlor of her father's mansion, and after a few moments of silence, the reverend gentleman spoke as follows :—

"Miss Priscilla! I have had something on my mind for a long time, I wish to communicate. I—ahem!—I believe I will say it now."

"Thank goodness! he is coming to the point at last," thought she. But her eyes were cast down, and her cheeks were ornamented with an orange colored blush.

"Miss Wiggins! Ahem! Miss Wiggins!" he began again, but there he paused, leaving her in a state of suspense, better imagined than described, for the space of five whole minutes, after which time he blew his nose and proceeded once more.

"In my calling, Miss Wiggins, I have become acquainted with many ladies, married and single, to whom I humbly trust I have been useful, in giving instruction on important subjects, but never before, I must say it, even though it seems like flattery, never before have I met with one who seemed so anxious to acquire knowledge, or whose zeal was so unremitting as yours appears to be, my dear Miss Priscilla."

Miss Wiggins raised her eyes, and looked unutterable things at her pastor.

"Consequently, having your good at heart," he continued, "I find myself, perhaps unwarrantably, settling a future for you. I picture you moving in the sphere for which you are the best fitted, and glory in the thought that I have led you to the path. My dear friend, will you listen to me and think seriously of my proposition?"

"Do proceed, sir," sighed Priscilla, covering her face with her kerchief to conceal the triumph in her eyes, "oh, *do* proceed, sir!"

"Among worldly people," continued the minister, "the pious mind allows itself to rest. My dear Miss Wiggins, unite your destiny with those who will appreciate you, and become"—a violent fit of coughing interrupted him—"become—ahem!"—

"Why *don't* he say 'my wife' and done with it?" thought Priscilla.

"Become," continued the reverend gentleman, "that which you are fitted for by every attribute of mind and heart. It is my nightly prayer, and I beg of you to consent to embark in the great cause, and go out to Hindostan as a missionary in the vessel which sails next week for that distant land. As a general thing, the female constitution can resist the climate for two years or more, and think of the good which you could accomplish in that length of time! Dear, dear Miss Wiggins! promise me that you will embrace the glorious opportunity!"

He paused, and for the first time in her life, Priscilla had really fainted.

Some weeks elapsed, and Miss Wiggins departed from Slab-town, and took up her residence in New York, where she opened a seminary, and became a professed man hater. According to her theory, there is neither faith nor gratitude in the whole sex, and the woman who trusts her heart to even the best man living, must be irretrievably ruined. At times, she attends Women's Rights Conventions, and has been known to give utterance to her sentiments from the rostrum ; and now and then she inflicts her presence upon the family of her younger brother, where her visits are dreaded as a pestilence. Men laugh at her, married ladies avoid her, and young girls abhor her. No where is she welcome save among a clique of strong-minded spinsters, who, like herself, amuse themselves, by saying ugly things about men.

* * * * * * *

There are a great many " man-haters" in New York, but they are not all as ill-featured as Miss Wiggins, for some are young and beautiful. Yet, when we hear a woman, old or young, denouncing the opposite sex, we at once conclude that there has been some little disappointment in their " cap setting" calculation. It is very foolish for women to talk bitterly about *all* men, because *one* has fallen short of their wishes or affections. It will do for such as Priscilla Wiggins, but those who have youth, and any claim to beauty, had much better laugh and be happy, than to hide away and get old and sour.

CYNTHIA DOLL.

CYNTHIA DOLL.

THE FASCINATING LADY.

She was fair—and my passion begun,
She smiled—and I could not but love;
She is faithless—and I am undone.—SHAKSPEARE.

ISS Doll belongs to a tolerably good family, and is at least rich enough to afford becoming garments, and all those little nameless additions to the toilette, which go so far to "make up" a good appearance. Her hair is always dressed in the latest style, and her hands are soft and white and skillfully displayed. Of course she can sing and dance and "play" the piano, and she understands the true use of a fan, in each and all its coquettish evolutions. No gentleman is safe in her society. If he has a heart, she discovers its vulnerable point, almost before the introduction is over. To a musical gentleman, she professes herself a worshiper of music, to an artist, a devotee of art. In the presence of a clergyman, there is nothing so interesting as the heathen, and with Young America, she will discuss "fast horses, and dashing turn-outs," with the greatest gusto. Her chief aim is a rich husband, but meanwhile *every* masculine comes in for a share of her attention, and he who has most pocket money, and can offer the most invitations to the opera, is decidedly the favorite. Miss Doll cultivates the acquaintance of other young ladies who have handsome and gallant brothers, or cousins, or even fathers who being widowers are still polite to pretty faces. Of all things, she loves a tete-a-tete, and when alone with any one who is worth the while, can look unutterable feelings whereby she impresses her companion with the belief that he is all the world to her. Her favorite songs are those which are the particularly sentimental, such as "Ever of Thee," "One kind kiss before we part." And the young gentleman who turns her music, is always certain that she is singing for him especially, while every other moustache in the room, is of the same decided opinion. Miss Doll knows by experience, that the first means of gaining the adoration of the sterner sex, is to privately feign unbounded admiration for each particular specimen, and to distribute universal smiles in public. Young ladies who are betrothed, and young wives who are blessed with susceptible husbands, are rather shy of encouraging visits from the fascinating young lady, for they know that man is a frail vessel, and that she is sure to make a dead set at anything in masculine habiliments, which comes within her orbit, from the boy in round-about, to the white headed old grandfather. Many and many a happy married life has been first broken in upon by a visit from Miss Doll, who will sing little bits from Norma while "wife" nurses the baby, and many a lover's quarrel has originated in a short visit on the part of the betrothed gentleman, to which he has been led on, by the smiles and coquetry of our charming heroine.

Miss Doll's drawers are filled with presents from her admirers—with fans, rings, breast pins, chains and opera glasses, books, boquet holders and perfumery, bracelets and card cases. All is fish which comes to her net, and she has a trophy of each and every conquest.

She is an adept in securing invitations, and always hints in the strongest manner, that she would "dearly love to hear" this Prima Donna, or that great actor. But the crowning glory of her life is the jealousy of other less attractive females. She loves to see them struggling to keep back the frown or to brush away the tear. She delights to see their admiration, and their unconsciously reproachful glances. She enjoys her triumph without the least shadow of remorse, no matter how deep the grief which

it occasions. Miss Doll will not marry very early, nor will she remain an old maid. Her choice, unless she delays too long and is obliged to take the crooked stick at last, is one who has plenty of money at his command, and is of an easy and amiable disposition. After her marriage she will continue to fascinate until grey hairs and wrinkles destroy her power, and then she'll dye the first, paint out the last, wear false teeth and plenty of padding. Then they will say she must have been exceedingly fascinating when she *was* younger.

* * * * * * *

"Fascinating Ladies" are very numerous in New York. The most of them are only spoiled daughters of moderately circumstanced parents who expected them to marry fortunes. Their education is generally the same smattering of useless affectations and nonsensical ideas. They seldom marry to good advantage after all. In truth, such women are totally unfit to assume the position of an exemplary wife, and it generally happens that they are either divorced a few years after marriage, or sink into a state of apathy which soon drives their husbands elsewhere for congenial society. Occasionally, a Fascinating Lady catches a rich spoony whom she can manage and control. In that case, she continues to have all her whims fully gratified until Mr. Spoony's fortune is exhausted, and the creditors carry off the carriage and the nice furniture. Then Spoony is very much in the way. He is entirely unnecessary now, and stands between her and better fortune. Yet Spoony is not so terribly formidable, and if her beauty still blooms, she may keep her head up awhile longer, with the kind assistance of a few particular friends. But Spoony is no longer in the horizon. He was never accustomed to employment or business, so he can now amuse himself at the lounges of the city, while she rides out with her particular friends, or goes with them to the opera or attends balls. "Fascinating Ladies" never have children, and that is truly kind in them, for the offspring of such mothers would have to abide with cross nurses and grow up in dismal boarding-schools, or run to destruction without maternal regard or control.

New York is the paradise of Fascinating Ladies.

AUNTY GREEN.

AUNTY GREEN:

THE OLD PEDDLER-WOMAN.

Ah me! what is there in earth's various range,
Which time and absence may not sadly change?—SANDS.

OLD Aunty Green calls at the basement doors, in the upper part of the city, almost every day, carrying her basket of tapes, candies, and brass thimbles in one hand, and leaning upon a cane for support with the other. She has a good, honest old face, crossed by many wrinkles, and shaded by the broad border of a thick muslin cap, beneath her little black bonnet, and her shoulders are wrapped in a queer plaid shawl, pinned over her bosom and knotted behind. Whoever speaks to her must purchase something from her slender stock, for she will tell such doleful stories, and importune so pitifully, that it is beyond human power to resist her pleadings. Out of that little basket, she says, must come food, fire, and clothing, for herself and her husband, and he, poor man, is old and sick, and blind, and can do nothing but sit at home.

"You are a good soul," she will say to you, "buy something from a poor old creature, who has been on her feet all day."

Perhaps, (if you are in a good humor) you not only buy some of those doubtful needles, and a skein or so of *that* frail thread, but you also ask her in to rest herself by the kitchen fire. Perhaps, you will tell Biddy to give her a cup of tea, and a slice of that pudding that was left from dinner. Then, when her heart is warmed by your kindness, she will become very talkative while she sips the fragrant tea, telling you of her own life, of her past joys and present sorrows.

"Ah! I've seen better days, ma'am," she will begin, "I never thought to come to peddling for a living. We were quite rich when we were hearty and young."

"Indeed!" you say, sympathizingly. "It must be hard for you to feel want now in your old age."

"Ah, indeed it is," she answers, "very hard. But we dread going to the poor house, and we can't bear to beg. What else could I do but peddle?"

You do not know what to say, so you shake your head and keep silent.

"It all came of our poor boy going a little wild," she continues. "He was a good boy, but you know that boys will be boys, and he was like the rest. Ah, it's very hard to raise boys. Have you any yourself, ma'am?"

If you are a mother, you will say yes, between a smile and a tear, as you think of your little innocent one in the cradle, and the two elder ones away at school.

"Ah, well, well!" the old lady answers, "God prosper you with them, for He only can say what their lives will be. And I feel He had a right to do what he chose with mine, for He gave him to me. But ah, it was a sore trouble to me, at that time."

You ask what she alludes to, and she pushes back her spectacles, and wipes her eyes with her blue checked apron.

"We named him John, after his grandfather, poor old man, and he grew up just as good and handsome as a boy could grow. He had pretty blue eyes, and flaxen hair, and as long as he went to school he was quick at his learning. He read like a school master, and his writing was just as black and sloping as it could be. Ah, I was proud of him. But then, it's natural to be proud of your own children, ain't it ma'am?"

Again you think of your own rosy cheeked little ones, and murmur, "Indeed it is—a mother can not help loving her own children."

"Ah, I couldn't," says the old woman, "nor his father, neither. Well, when he was quite grown up, we put him to learn a trade. The carpenter's trade, ma'am, with a very good master. He came to see us regular every Sunday, and made us very happy for a long time. But one day he came in looking so dull and moody that I scarcely knew him; and when I said to him, 'What's the matter, John? has the boss been hard to please or angry?' he turned to me, and said he,—'Mother, I wish to heaven I'd never gone away from home. I wish I was a little boy again, as good and innocent as I used to be!' and he laid his head in my lap and cried like a baby. After that, ma'am, I knew something dreadful had happened; and when his master came to tell us that he had robbed him, I was not so astonished as his father, though it was a dreadful thing to hear."

"And what led him to the act?" you ask.

It was all owing to his making bad acquaintances," she answers, "and to the influence of a designing, wicked woman. That's what it was that ruined my poor boy. Well, ma'am, his father sold all our property to pay for what he'd taken, rather than have him punished, and he went away to sea; and the last words I heard him say, were—'Mother, if ever I come back again, I'll work for you in your old age, and be an honest man from this time forth!' Ah, poor fellow, he never came back!"

"Was he lost?" you inquire.

"Yes, ma'am," sobs the poor old woman, "the ship was wrecked, and he was drowned; and the last words he said were these:—'Tell mother my thoughts shall be of her until I die.'"

You feel very kindly to the old peddler as she rises to go. She slips the pudding into her basket by stealth, that she may take it home to her old husband.

"May God bless you, ma'am, and may you never want a good home!" she says as she turns away.

You will watch her, as she carries her little basket down the street, and wonder why fortune's favors are so unfairly divided, and why so many bad people are rich, and so many good ones poor.

But all peddlers are not good and honest, like old Aunty Green. Where there is one to be trusted, there are a dozen who will cheat you, and perhaps steal when you turn your back. There is one particular class of peddlers which none feel any sympathy for. We allude to an unprincipled fraternity of Jewesses, who carry large baskets of fanciful gilt china vases, and little cups and saucers, and cologne bottles, which they desire to "trade" for old clothes. They are so very impudent, that hardly any hostility, short of a kick or a push, will drive them away. Whoever trades with one of these Jewesses must get cheated, and it is advisable to keep them out of the house.

Some years ago, there was a little old woman, shriveled to a mere skeleton, and almost bent double, who nearly every day sat on a stone step in Chatham street, with a very little basket of peanuts by her side. She trembled and waddled so in all her limbs, that she could scarcely touch or hold any thing in her hands. Her countenance was the most aged one we had ever seen, and in curiosity and pity we inquired her history.

"Go along, young woman!" replied a squeeking voice, hardly above a whisper, "don't be making fun of me. You'll be old yourself some day, if you live as long as I have. Go away, and the sun will shine on me, for I'm very cold."

We had some difficulty to convince her that we did not wish to ridicule her, but that kind feelings prompted our inquiries. After quite a pause, during which she gazed in our face as steadfast and as straight as her trembling neck would permit her, she deigned to speak.

"Ugh! well, then may be you ain't like the rest of them. Ah, you have blue eyes. I used to have blue eyes, too, but alack, they are red eyes now." She tried to smile as she said this, but the deep wrinkles would not relax, and her countenance remained rigid. "When I was young, I thought blue eyes were truthful, but, oh dear, I've seen enough since then to make me believe there is not much in the color of eyes, any how. Yet, I like you all the better for having blue eyes. You want to know how old I am? Oh, I'm considerably past a hundred."

"Were you always poor?" we inquired.

"No. I have lived in grand style during three periods of my life. I had four husbands before I was thirty. The first deserted me, the second disappeared suddenly, and was afterwards found drowned, the third was thrown from a horse and killed, and the last fell dead in the street from apoplexy. I never had any children, and have no relations in this city. I live in a garret, in Mott street. People drop pennies and silver into my lap and into my basket as they pass, and in that way I get plenty to pay my rent, and buy my bread and tea, and snuff."

At this juncture she produced a leather bag of snuff, and offered us a "pinch," but we declined. She then rubbed a handful into her nose, and was silent. Not having time to remain longer, we left, intending to talk with her again some other day; but we never saw her there after that.

One cold morning in the winter of fifty-six and fifty-seven, a tremulous female voice, at the door of our sanctum, meekly begged us to buy "just a little bit of the nicest soap in the world, at only sixpence a cake." The soap was wretched stuff, and we declined with a sharp negative. "Oh, do, madame," urged the voice in choking accents, "do buy one piece. I am very poor, and my three little children haven't tasted a bit of bread these two days." We looked up into the woman's face. Tears were in her swollen red eyes, and we felt sure that she told the truth. Giving her a piece of silver, we inquired where she lived, intending to send her relief. She withdrew, and we were happy in the thought that we had done a good act. But, later in the day, we discovered that she had stolen from us an embroidered handkerchief, a fine black veil, a scarf, and a pair of gold cuff pins.

MARY BROWN.

MARY BROWN,

THE MECHANIC'S WIFE.

Don't search for "an angel" a minute;
For granting you win in the sequel,
The deuce, after all, would be in it,
With a union so very "unequal."—SAXE.

MRS. BROWN'S father was a mechanic. She has always lived in New York, and would not voluntarily take up her residence elsewhere. In her opinion, Gotham is the greatest city on the face of the globe. She declares there is no street in the world like Broadway, no markets like Washington market, no church like Grace church, and no dry goods store like Lord & Taylor's. She turns up her nose at London, sneers at Philadelphia, scorns Boston, and fairly laughs at Washington. Mrs. Brown often regrets that she married a mechanic. She feels a desire to live in more fashionable style. As it is, she saves in the bread and butter, economizes the soup, does entirely without puddings, and makes pancakes without eggs, in order to keep up appearances. Her "Caroline Matilda" and her "Mary Emma," must both wear garments of the same cut and material as those adopted by millionaires' daughters. Yet, at the same time, Mrs. Brown is perfectly willing to stow herself and family into the least possible portion of a dwelling shared by several other families, and will subject herself to the inconvenience and injury of dark, unventilated bedrooms, and an underground dining-room, merely to save so much a year for finery in dress.

Living in part of a house has made Mrs. Brown cunning in the hiding away of surplus furniture and garments, and in the arrangement of concealed sleeping places. The shining bureau in the dining-room is really a bedstead, turned up by day and spread out by night. The moreen covered lounge, divested of its tassels and cushion, accommodates little Kitty, when that interesting infant seeks repose. The large haircloth armchair has a depository beneath the cushion, in which frying-pans, gridirons and saucepans are secreted. The "best tea set" is kept in a trunk under a bed, and an imposing ottoman, covered with crimson, is nothing more than a receptacle for the soiled linen of the family. Wonders can be done with the stove. The top may be removed, a graceful urn detached, and fixtures and conveniences revealed for the purpose of preparing the dinner. Behind the door of her bedroom, you will find a hoop skirt, hanging on a gimlet; outside of the window, on the roof of the back porch, are two tubs, a pail, and a bag of clothes-pins; and in the room where "the girl" sleeps, you may find coal and kindling-wood, blacking brushes and brooms, barrels and boxes, all mixed up in the most marvellous manner, and the girl's wearing apparel scattered about among them. Speaking of "the girl," she is inevitably Irish, and addicted to the wearing of plaid shawls and pink aprons. In addition to her daily routine of washing, ironing and scrubbing, she is expected to bring the news of the neighborhood to her mistress. It is "the girl" who discovers that Miss Smith is to be married, or that the grocer's wife is "too intimate" with her next door neighbor; that the Simpkinses have not paid the butcher, and that the dressmaker has sent her little bill to the Haddock's five times, without the least success. Over the ironing table, Mrs. Brown and "the girl" discuss these important topics, and hatch new scandal to be disseminated to the great discomfiture of some unhappy and often innocent neighbor. Now and then—say three times a year—the servant is dismissed. Sometimes she has "sassed" her mistress,—sometimes she has been found with her fingers in the jar of preserves, and occasionally she is suspected of appropriating other people's property. There is quite a commotion at her departure, and much slamming of doors. Mrs. Brown remarks aloud that she "never found any good in the Irish, and never expects to," and "the girl" flings back a hint to the effect that "she could tell things, if she would, and that she has seen enough in *that* house." Then Mrs. Brown flies at her with a broom, or the poker, and drives her ignominiously down stairs, and out of the front door, and falls into hysterics on one of the hall chairs, and is surrounded by all the other inmates of the house, who administer sympathy and cold water in equal quantities, and remark to each other that "girls are such a trial, and that, for their parts, if they were only strong, they wouldn't keep one." Finally, Mrs. Brown, somewhat composed, retires to her own apartments, administers correction to her small family, and a slapping to Billy, who took to pounding on a tin kettle in the height of the rumpus. She next dresses herself in her black silk, and locking the children up in the back room, with strict injunctions not to meddle with the fire nor fall out of the window, she goes away to spend the afternoon in calling upon some dear friends, and relating the terrible adventure she had that morning with "the girl." Of course, Mrs. Brown's spouse is a mechanic. He rises at five in the morning, and retires at nine in the evening,—comes home to dinner at twelve, and takes tea at seven. His only earthly happiness consists in working for enough to feed himself, Mrs. Brown and the children. The only recreation he gets is on Sunday, which he spends in taking short naps, or sitting on the doorstep in his best coat, and occasionally quarreling with his neighbors. He reads the political articles in the daily papers, and makes a point of drinking too much, and voting at every election for some one of whom he knows nothing.

Mrs. Brown does not spend *her* Sundays in napping. Early on the morning of that day she is dressed in her best, and proceeds, rain or shine, to public worship, as often as is practicable. The minister is her special object of adoration. Together with the other lady members of his flock, she makes a pet of him. She sends him currant jelly for his sore throat, and hems cravats and 'kerchiefs for him,—invites him to tea, and wishes that poor dear Brown would sit under him and be edified. Sometimes, at church, she offers up a prayer for the unconverted Brown, and feeling sure that she has done her duty, she satisfies herself that Mrs. Smith's bonnet is only turned and made over—as is plain to be seen in a bright light.

At charitable collections, Mrs. Brown is foremost in everything but giving money. She delights to play colporteur whenever she has an opportunity, as it affords her such an excellent chance to pry into people's dwellings and investigate the private life of strangers. In company with some other zealous lady, Mrs. Brown will sally out, armed with fifty copies of "Bob, the Cabin Boy," and penetrating into tenant houses, she will inquire of their occupants whether they ever go to church, and how long they have been married; whether they ever think of their souls, and how much they earn a week; whether they will come and hear Mr. Jobkins next Sabbath, and whether they paid the rent where they lived last.

Next to tract distributing, Mrs. Brown most enjoys having company to tea. Over the cakes and preserves, characters are torn to tatters. Stories which have grown, like snowballs in the course of rolling, from one social gathering to another, are augmented by being handed around the circle, and before the pleasant meeting breaks up, you cannot hear of one virtuous and respectable woman or man within twenty miles.

* * * * * * * *

Such are some of the peculiarities of Mrs. Brown. But there are *other* mechanics' wives who do not see so happy a time. Some mechanics earn poor wages, and are themselves poor, not only in purse, but in skill and habits of industry. The wives of such must necessarily live in miserable garrets, and sometimes want comforts beyond their reach. The higher class of mechanics receive from ten to twenty dollars per week, and if their wives are prudent and economical, they may get along quite snugly. Though it often happens that mechanics' wives are ignorant slatterns, who were raised in workshops or in idle poverty, and then, no matter how much wages the husbands may earn, their abodes show only squalid discomfort. Thus it is that so many mechanics spend their evenings and their earnings in lager beer saloons, and play dominoes and cards and chess and billiards, until they become inebriated, and lose their work, and go down to vagrancy and to crime. On the other hand, a worthy and industrious wife can reclaim a drunken husband, and encourage him to struggle through labor and to toil with ambition until he gains wealth and position. Many instances are known of mechanics acquiring fame and fortune with energy and resolution inspired and sustained by good and exemplary wives. Though in New York, we believe that there are more instances of wives ruining their husbands, than of helping them up to any honorable distinction. Next to ignorance, we may mention laziness as a sad bane among artizan's wives. Then when vanity steps in to abide with a lazy woman, she is no helpmate for a laboring man ; and if she has a very pretty face, he may return from his daily labor to find himself a widower, with two or three small children to nurse and put to bed, while their mother tries her fortune in another position of life, where there is a better prospect of luxury and show. It has been estimated by a wise head, that in New York, at least one mechanic's wife in every ten who have pretty faces, voluntarily divorces herself for fine clothes and dissipation. It is said that the wives of men in humble circumstances are most noted for their virtue ; but laziness, vanity, novel-reading and a pretty face, are doubtful safeguards for purity in any sphere of life.

HELEN BRAY.

HELEN BRAY:

THE BALLET GIRL.

Think not, because the eye is bright,
And smiles are laughing there,
The heart that beats within is light,
And free from pain and care.

Appearances may deceive thee—understand,
A pure white dress may hide a guilty heart.
Where mincing dancers sport tight pantalets,
And turn fops' heads while turning pirouetts.

AN airy vision seems to rise before your eyes, and you see a beautiful creature all grace and brightness, floating in the radiance of the golden gas light to the sound of joyous music. She is rosy cheeked with happiness, and radiant with smiles, and you cannot divest yourself of the idea that she dances because she loves to. Even when you know that she does it to earn her bread and butter, you still fancy that she must feel light hearted and happy. The painted scene, through which she glides, looks like a garden of living flowers ; but, alas! her smiles and the blossoms are not real. They live but for the eye of the spectator. Behind the scenes, they turn to rouged cheeks and tinseled canvass.

The ballet girl *at home*, is a very different being from the fairy queen, who flourishes her gilded scepter upon the stage.

When you see a ballet girl executing her capricious phantasies with so much ease, call to mind what it has cost her to arrive at so much perfection—a cost not only of labor, but of real suffering.

At six, she is placed under the care of some good dancing master, who never pauses before the means of achieving an effectual result. Every morning when the class is opened, the poor child's feet are *placed*, the heels together, and the toes pointing outwards in a straight line, in slits, in the floor, made expressly for the purpose. She cries at first, her face is distorted by misery, but it is in vain, she must submit.

After a month's training, she can turn her feet without the machine of torture. Then begins the posturing exercise, which consists of efforts, seemingly impossible at first, to bend the loins across a bar, and then, unaided, regain an upright position. Fresh cries, tears, and sufferings. Pshaw! it is nothing to the initiated. She is solaced by the assurance that all the world will drag her in a triumphal car some day.

At last, the loins have become supple; she can spring, pirouette, or bound twenty times a minute, without being out of breath, or run on her toes, or do a dozen equally wonderful things, and smile all the while.

Ten years she has spent at this violent teaching, and now at sixteen, she enters a *corps de ballet*, as one of the minor members. She walks behind the others, on the third row, receiving $3 a week, and finds most of her own costumes. Her mother, (they all have mothers,) is ever beside her, watching and hoping. One day, the third best *danseuse* is ill; the unknown girl is called upon to fill her place for the night. She fulfills her task to the satisfaction of the director; she has been noticed. Another time the second *danseuse* is absent; she replaces her with complete success; and, as a crowning triumph, a something or other calls upon her one night to take the first part in the ballet, and audaciously and admirably she does it. Her mother takes three pinches of snuff extra, (all the mothers of ballet girls take snuff,) in proof that her dreams are realized.

She thereupon quits her garret where she and her daughter had existed, and takes an apartment on the second floor. As her child rises in the world, she descends the stairs.

Nevertheless, the *ex-figurant*, who has become a celebrity of the first-class, continues her practicings, as before, at home, to preserve her suppleness and activity; she worked to obtain them; she must now work not to lose them. Every gesture is studied before a glass. She bends backwards, bounds, stoops, springs upwards, and flits like a bird from branch to branch, and when she requires a *little repose from her labors*, amuses herself by twisting round a triangle!

She flies from one city to another; and if she succeeds, as only one in a thousand do, she will realize a fortune either by her profession or by catching a very rich, and of course, very silly husband.

There are two sorts of talents in a *danseuse*—to be a good pantomimist and one whose dancing alone possesses merit. When a girl unites the two, it is ensuring success doubly. This is Madame Rosati's secret, in which none surpass her.

Ballet dancing often saves a bad opera. We have heard of an instance in which a manager was in great distress because his opera did not draw.

"Oh," said a wise friend, "You must shorten the Ballet girl's petticoats!"

The manager did so, and the opera was saved. In Paris, at the time of the Restoration, a nobleman, whose business it was to regulate all matters appertaining to the Fine Arts, restored the ballerines' petticoats to their former length, and the public deserted the place, which, to revenge themselves, they nicknamed "The Moral Academy of Music." More recently, in Naples, the ballet dancers were forced to dance in any ordinary dress. Of course the receipts at the theatre diminished amazingly, and the director is using all his interest to obtain permission to curtail the offending dresses which now sweep his boards.

* * * * * * *

Hush! It is midnight, and the theatres are closed. Look yonder, and see that female form hurrying along the street. She is shabbily attired, and carries a large bundle. Look at her again, for you saw her only an hour ago, in very different guise. She is one of the ballet girls, who filled the stage of the theatre in the fairy pantomime. She danced well, and was so very bewitching in her character of a romping school girl. But, ah! her real life is a weary one. When "made up" on the stage, with aid of ribbons, gause, false curls, a gay costume, and pearl powder and vinegar rouge, she will appear to be not more than sixteen, and as beautiful as an angel; but she is past twenty-five, and by day light, in her plain clothes, she might be taken for thirty-five—perhaps forty! You would not recognize her in the street, after seeing her on the stage, as she looks for all the world like a grandmother, instead of the beautiful Helen Bray.

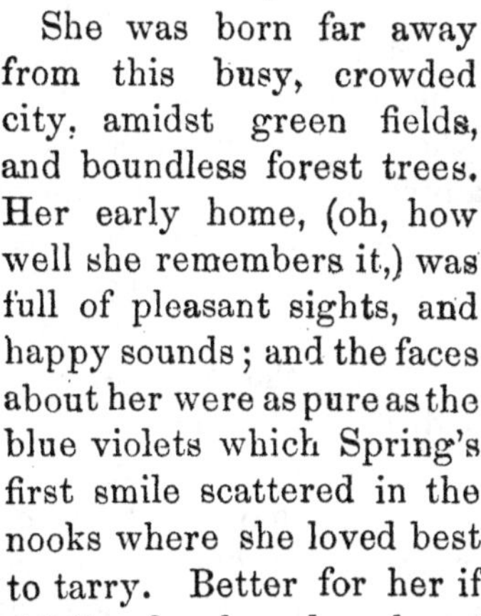

She was born far away from this busy, crowded city, amidst green fields, and boundless forest trees. Her early home, (oh, how well she remembers it,) was full of pleasant sights, and happy sounds; and the faces about her were as pure as the blue violets which Spring's first smile scattered in the nooks where she loved best to tarry. Better for her if she had died in childhood, when her heart was full of joy, before she knew even the dread name of sin. Helen's father was a poor man, but an unexpected legacy from an old relative, turned his steps towards the city. Despite the earnest pleadings of his wife, he resolved to forsake the ploughshare, and invest his little fortune in some business in the metropolis. But when honest simplicity is matched against craft and cunning, the former invariably becomes the dupe of the latter, and so Helen's father soon found himself penniless in the midst of strangers. In despair, he took to drink, and sank lower and lower, until he became entirely debased and brutal. Poor Helen was the eldest daughter, and she sought in vain for employment, which might save them from starvation. She was naturally apt in dancing and very pretty, and at last, following the suggestions of an actor, succeeded in obtaining a situation as supernumerary at the Old Bowery Theatre. The salary which she receives, is barely enough to keep the family alive. She endures huffs and scoldings innumerable from the manager, and is looked upon with disdain by those who have attained a higher position. Her nights are passed upon the stage, her days in attending rehersals, and manufacturing the gaudy dresses in which she makes her appearance ; and even the repose she gets, is broken by the curses of her degraded father, and the wailing of the unhappy children, upon whom his angry blows have fallen. From scenes of misery and suffering, with an aching heart, and a brain too often burning with the insults which she has received from those who take advantage of her exposed and unprotected situation, poor Helen Bray, like many of her sisters, comes upon the stage to dance and smile. and entertain the public world.

Is it any wonder that Helen Bray should listen to the tempter, who comes with bright yellow gold? Her mother died long ago, and her father is now utterly depraved. Poor Helen! She might have been a good woman, honest and pure, if her father had not brought her to this great Sodom, and forced her into the slough of perdition.

MARTHA BENTON.

MARTHA BENTON:

THE TRUE WOMAN.

I am not *old*—tho' Time has set
  His signet on my brow,
And some faint furrows there have met,
  Which care may deepen now;
For in my heart a fountain flows,
And round it pleasant thoughts repose,
And sympathies and feelings high,
Spring like stars on even sky.

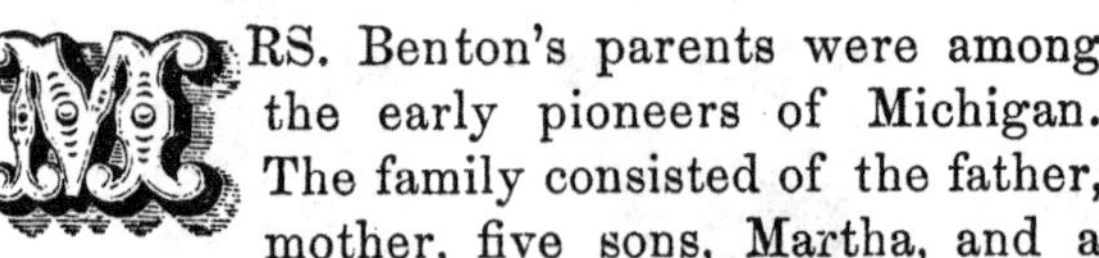

MRS. Benton's parents were among the early pioneers of Michigan. The family consisted of the father, mother, five sons, Martha, and a babe, just beginning to crawl. They, with a hired man, were the only human beings upon the little clearing, and for miles upon either side no feet, save those of the red man, ever awakened the silence. Martha, as the largest girl, had her hands full; it was her task to make the butter and mind the baby, mend the stockings, milk the cows, feed the chickens, and teach her young brothers and sisters their letters. Her hands spun the yarn, picked the geese, washed all the chubby faces, and cut all the tremendous slices of bread and butter which were consumed between meals by the hearty urchins. She it was to whom Tom came when he cut his finger, and to whom Dick brought his dilapidated waistcoat for repairs; and her hands were always busy, and ever ready for additional tasks.

By good farming, and the sale of skins and furs, the father had laid by a clever number of hard silver dollars, which he kept piled upon the narrow shelf of a tall cupboard, at one side of the chimney; and as food cost nothing but labor, and as finery was never even thought of, these piles of dollars were increasing with each succeeding year. There were no thieves in those regions, and the closet had not even a lock upon the door, precious as were its contents. As for the main entrance, there was a bar to that, but it was rather to keep out the old cow, who had a habit of lifting the latch and walking in unexpectedly, than for any purpose of safety; for the little family, in their loneliness, were strangers to fear and apprehension.

One day in autumn, the old man and his sons

set off for a day's hunting, and the mother went to the nearest village to do a little trading, and visit some old and long neglected friends.

Martha was left alone with the little ones. She put the house to rights, combed all the children's round, white heads, and sat down with her knitting upon the rude porch, just as the noonday sun glittered upon the water of the pretty lake in front of the door, where the white geese were sporting and splashing. The children, who had already eaten their dinner, were at a wild game of romps in the kitchen, and Martha, growing lonesome, was just wishing for some companion, when she descried a dark figure crossing the opposite field and approaching the house. "Who can it be?" thought Martha, dropping her knitting. "It does not look like any one we know."

He was a large man, attired in rough garments, and with a sun-burnt face, which told of much exposure to wind and weather, and she noticed that he eyed the house curiously as he approached. He stopped beside the porch, when he had reached it, and requested rest and entertainment, in the rough language of a woodsman. Such an application was never refused in those days and in that region, and Martha requested the stranger to walk in. She soon spread the board with a cold meal, substantial as it was plentiful. The man seated himself, and plied his knife and fork vigorously. His appetite satisfied, and having swallowed a pitcher of buttermilk, he backed his chair against the wall and addressed himself to Martha.

"How's the old man, and the rest of 'em?"

"They're very well," replied Martha. "Father and Tom and Dick have gone a hunting, and Mother and Dave have driven to Dexter to do some trading. I didn't think you knew them."

"Oh, yes, I've seen the old man and the boys very often," replied the stranger. "So you're all alone, are you? Don't you feel skittish?"

"Not a bit of it," replied Martha. "What should I feel skittish about?"

"Stragglers or Injuns, I reckon," replied the man.

"None of 'em ever come to these parts," said Martha.

"But jist supposin', for the fun of it, that one of them fellers *was* to come, and ask you to fork over the old man's dollars, what would you allow to do *then*, gal?"

"I'd allow to shoot him through the head, if he didn't go faster than he came," said Martha.

"You would!" ejaculated the stranger. "But

I reckon two could play at that game, if he had a couple of these *here* about him." As he spoke he drew two pistols from his belt. "What would you do when they was pointed towards you, hay?"

"I'd—I hardly know—but I'm sure I'd do *something*," said Martha, half amused and half frightened.

"Try to think, gal, for between you and I and the post, I'd like you to hand over them dollars the old man has stowed somewhere about the house. You're all alone, remember, so the better you mind the better you'll find yourself when we are done."

Martha sprang towards the spot where an old rifle hung, but the stranger was too quick for her, and stood laughing before it.

"Jest look for them there dollars, my dear, will you?"

"I don't know where they are," answered Martha.

"Yes, you do. Come, I'm not to be trifled with. Speak out, or I'll send a bullet through that obstinate head of yours."

Martha's blood ran cold, but she was resolved to protect her father's property if she had strength or ingenuity to do so, and she rapidly glanced over the room, to see what means of resistance lay within her reach. Her eyes lighted on a trap-door, which was the only entrance to a small cellar beneath the house. Once there, and the door shut upon him, she believed that she could prevent his egress until her father's return. The children had wandered down near the brook, and Martha glanced towards them. Perhaps it was her last look, she thought; and then, turning to the man beside her, she said,

"Well, as you say, I'm *alone*, and I reckon you are the strongest. The money is in a stone jar, in the cellar, but if Dad ever finds out I told you, it will be the worse for me. If you want it, you'll have to go down and get it yourself."

"Aye! I'll go down fast enough," said the ruffian. "But you must go with me, my gal. You can't come any of your tricks over me. I keep my eyes open, I do. Come along." And as he spoke, he set one foot on the upper step of the trap-way.

Martha's heart beat furiously. Only a few moments remained for action. She applied her apron to her eyes and feigned to weep.

"Wait until I light a candle, the cellar is awful dark," she sobbed, and turning towards a shelf as she spoke, she took down a heavy iron candlestick, in which an end still remained. Lighting it, she advanced towards the ruffian.

Her hand trembled so that the light flared and flickered, and the melted grease dropped down upon her little fingers. The robber noticed this, and taking it for terror, descended another step, and looked down into the cellar, with a brutal grin upon his features. As he did so, Martha hurled the iron candlestick straight at his head. There was a crash and groan, and the heavy form slipped from its narrow foothold, and fell, like a lump of lead, upon the ground beneath. In an instant the trap-door was closed, and Martha jumped on top of it. She wiped the cold dew from her forehead, and listened with. fear for any sound which should tell of the robber returning to consciousness.

It was well the blow had been so heavy, and the fall so great. It was well, indeed, for Martha, that he lay stunned and bleeding, unable to rise or speak, for her little weight could never have held the door down against him. When she could recover her breath, she called her little brothers to help her keep the trap-door down, fearing that the prisoner might force it up. One of the little fellows, of his own accord, ran and got the hammer and some nails, and she soon fastened the entrance securely enough. Then, for the first time, she gave way to a flood of girlish tears.

The weary afternoon was slow in passing, but twilight brought the farmer and his sons back to their lonely dwelling. Great was their astonishment to discover what had transpired during their absence, and great the old farmer's gratitude to his daughter for her courage and presence of mind which had saved his hard-earned dollars. In a little while the prisoner was brought forth, and bound, and when the wagon brought Martha's mother back from the village, it was once more put in requisition to convey him to the nearest jail.

So courageous a girl, naturally made a brave, good woman.

Martha was married early, and came with her husband to the city of New York, where they continued to live many years, prosperous and respected, establishing their sons in various professions, and seeing their daughters well and happily settled in life.

Her husband died long ago, leaving her still in good health.

In the old dwelling, where they lived together for so many years, she continues to reside, loved and honored by a score and a half of grandchildren. She is not particularly fashionable or stylish, but her dwelling is large and grand, and we wish there were more women like her.

LILLIE BELL.

LILLIE BELL:

THE FEMALE WRITER.

Some write, confined by physic; some, by debt;
Some for 'tis Sunday; some, because 'tis wet;
Another writes because his father writ,
And proves himself a bastard by his wit.—YOUNG.

LILLIE Bell's *real* name is plain Ruth Flatfoot. She resides in the city of New York, and inflicts her presence upon the family of her married sister. She is an old maid, whose human kindness seems to have turned to gall. She hates every one who is happy or good looking, and especially pretty girls, because their beauty attracts the attention of those masculine eyes, which she has so long and so vainly endeavored to draw upon her own charms. She hates young mothers, because they are married, and she has never been. She hates old ladies, because they seem to rejoice in the affection of their sons and daughters. She hates little girls, because they may eventually grow up to be pleasing women. She hates men, because they disregard her merits. Ruth is seldom seen at home without a pen between her fingers, and various ink stains upon the bony knuckles of her right hand. She writes articles for the papers, and is very bitter on the faults of poor human nature. Sometimes, in her more tender moods, she attempts sentimental poetry, and introduces love and a tombstone. Her heroes are in perpetual despair, and her heroines all die. Her chamber would strike terror to the heart of any good housekeeper. Old ink bottles cover the tables, quires of scribbled foolscap lay upon the carpet, and magazines and pamphlets without number, are tumbling out of place, and sticking between the hinges of half shut closet doors. Her wardrobe appears to have been tossed into the drawers of her beureau with a pitch fork, and every article of her attire is stained with ink. Her cloak, hanging on a peg behind the door, still bears the label which the shop man placed upon it to attract attention. The label reads thus :—" Very fashionable—only five dollars !"

It is her chief boast that people are afraid of her. She glories in making sharp speeches, and hitting people in the tenderest points ;

and after inflicting a mental stab, always closes her thin lips, with an air which plainly says, "See what it is to be a smart woman!"

When any lady is spoken of in her presence as being pretty, she assumes a scornful glance, and remarks, "Pretty enough, but, dear me, not at all *intellectual;*" or, "She may have fine eyes, but, then her mind—good gracious!—give me a woman with a *mind.*" As for the gentlemen, she has a list of dreadful anecdotes to relate about them.

Mr. Sykes drinks too much. Mr. Bingham flirts with young ladies. Mr. Trotters neglects his wife for a designing widow, and Mr. Harrowbones has cheated all his creditors. In short, her heart is as ill favored as her face, and her actions invariably correspond. No one will ever love her, or feel friendship for her, and she cares for no creature save herself. While living she will never be esteemed, and she will not be regretted when she dies.

* * * * * * * *

Our business necessarily brings us into contact with many female writers who figure in the periodicals, and we must say, that with half a dozen exceptions, Ruth Flatfoot, *alias* "Lillie Bell," is a very fair type of the most of them.

Some are ridiculous in manners, dress, and

speech. A few are down-right repulsive. There is one in particular, whose complexion is suggestive of buttermilk and sour curds. She does all kinds of "pieces," for any body who will *pay* her for them, and undertake the trouble and labor of preparing them for type. Her literary forte seems to be in the use and arrangement of dyspeptic adjectives, and asthmatical adverbs. Her principal characters are school girls, old women, and cats. She claims to have studied grammar at the seminary, but being now a widow, its use is totally unnecessary. She is addicted to cold cream externally, and hates soap and water. We always feel qualmish when she approaches. She is forever boring you to *read* her stories, and asks you what you think they are worth. If you reject them, or allude to any of their countless defects, she flounts out, and goes away to hate you forever.

KATE RAYMOND.

KATE RAYMOND;

THE OUTCAST WIFE.

Once I was pure as the snow, but I fell!
Fell, like a snow-flake, from heaven to hell!
Fell, to be trampled as filth in the street,
Fell, to be scoffed, to be spit on, and beat;
Pleading, cursing, dreading to die;
Selling my soul to whoever would buy;
Dealing in shame for a home and for bread,
I hate the living, and fly from the dead.
Merciful God! *have* I fallen so low?
I, who was once as pure as the snow?
Once I was loved for my innocent grace,
Admired and sought for my charming face;
But love, respect, friends, husband—all,
God and myself, I have lost by my fall!

KATE RAYMOND was nursed amid green fields, and her playthings were acorns and butter-cups. The south wind sang her cradle-song, and the warbling of birds was the first sound that greeted her awakening ear. Amid these scenes

of rural life, she grew up as innocent and beautiful as a wild rose.

Kate, fortunately, had a good old grandmother, who, to use her own expression, believed in *bringing* children up, and not letting them run wild, like weeds; and, accordingly, she was drilled in domestic duties from early infancy. She was taught to be tidy before she could speak, and even in the cradle would stop crying at the word of command. Yet a merrier, happier child, never chased the butterflies, for judicious discipline is not cruelty, and good children, like good grown people, are always the happiest. Of course Kate went to school, and there learned to read, write, and cipher,—to work a sampler, and perform wonders in overhanding, stitching, and hemming. She learned to dance, and went to singing-school once in a week, and sang in the choir of the village church beside, for the practice of music. Kate's grandmother took charge of her home education, and the result was greatly to the old lady's credit.

As Kate grew older and taller, the young men of the place began to discover her perfections, and being sensible young farmers, preferred her homely accomplishments to an indifferent performance upon a cracked piano, or the embroidering of deformed dogs and pink faced shepherdesses upon perforated cardboard. Consequently, Kate found herself a rural belle at the dawning of her sixteenth year. All the other girls envied her, but they could not harm her. The richest young farmer in the place worshiped her, the young doctor who owned real estate in New York was at her feet, the lawyer's son would have died for her, and as for the minister, who was a widower, she might have married him at any moment,—not to mention a dozen others, well to do and handsome, among whom Kate might have taken her choice. Why, from them all, she should have selected young Richard Bruce, who was not only poor, but, being an orphan, had no expectations, and was certainly far from being an Apollo in form or person, was best known to herself.

Kate and Richard were betrothed, and when the fact became manifest, by those numberless little signs and tokens with which all my fair readers are perfectly *au fait*, there was quite a commotion. The young men were indignant, and the girls delighted, while old farmers and their wives shook their heads, and said what a foolish match it was, and how much better she might have married. Kate herself seemed very happy, and the cooking and sewing went on more briskly than before, for she should be a wife sometime, and these were the first duties of a poor man's help-mate, as grandma had often told her. When the evening set in, and Richard Bruce sat beside her upon the porch, or they walked together, arm in arm, through the clover, she thought how she would lighten every care of his existence, instead of looking forward (as many a betrothed girl does) to the time when he should toil to supply her with luxuries, while she folded her hands in idleness. But suddenly her quiet happiness was broken in upon. Richard was going to sea, an old relative, a sea captain, had offered him unusual advantages in a position on board his vessel, and with his future union with Kate in mind, he could not but accept the offer.

The ship was ready, the crew and cargo on board, and Kate and her old grandmother went down with Richard to see him off. There was a last, lingering kiss, a painful smothering of sighs, the waving of a snowy 'kerchief, and he was gone. In a little while, only a distant speck upon the water remained in sight, and at last even that had vanished. Slowly Kate went home to the old farm-house, desolated to her eyes now that he would no longer cross its threshold.

One change often seems to bring others in its train. A quiet life once broken, will break and break again, until the links which were so dear are swept away forever. Thus it was with Kate. Even while her first grief was fresh upon her, more bitter sorrows came to claim her tears, and teach her what a weary world this is. In three months from Richard's departure a fever swept the place, and left Kate an orphan. Her father was called away too suddenly to make arrangements which were needful, and one of those villains who are always prowling about the world upon Satan's errands, took advantage of his death to rob the orphan of her heritage. Raymond farm became the home of strangers, and Kate and her old grandmother were sent forth into the world to earn their bread. In all that bitter time which followed, there was but one ray of comfort, and that was the thought of Richard. His letters, precious as so many jewels to those stricken hearts, came at regular intervals, and brought hope and consolation with them. Best of all, he would return soon, and then he and Kate would never—*never* part again.

Death! Oh, that was a fearful word! and one dark, stormy night, when the wind rattled Kate's little window, and howled and moaned through the branches of the great oak tree which shadowed their humble dwelling, she prayed, tearfully, for that gallant ship, out upon the foaming billows.

A storm at sea! Dear reader, perhaps you saw an account of it in the papers, and spoke to your companions of the dismantled wreck, swept by the cruel tempest of all its crew, save one dead man, whose fingers were frozen fast to the rigging; and you may have remarked that the ship was supposed, by those who saw her, to be the "*Jenny Lind.*" But there was no word in the papers of the young sailor, Richard Brace, who must have perished with the doomed vessel on that fatal night; yet Kate read his name, in letters of blood, all over the paper which brought the news, and she sank to the floor, screaming, "He is *dead!*" Her voice did not seem to be her own, it was so wild and hollow.

Great grief seldom kills, it only scars and sears the future life, and, in a little while, Kate was well again, and working with her needle at her daily task. People said Richard was dead, and strove to comfort and console the sorrowing girl; but they whispered among themselves, "She is so young that her grief will be over in a little while, and some of these days she will make a better match."

In her day dreams, poor Kate saw that ship, tossed by the tempest and drifting before the wind, with that dead man frozen fast to the shattered rigging ; and in the night she would awaken, with a cry of horror, as Richard's face, white and rigid, with water dripping from his heavy ebon hair, rose above the water to torture her.

It was midwinter, and both food and fuel were very dear, and Kate's little hands must earn all they needed. The poor girl's life was one of unremitting toil, but she scarcely thought of that, her bitter sorrow lay so heavy at her heart. When presents came to the cottage, from some unknown friend, she scarcely glanced at them, and only remembered them with a shudder, for her woman's instinct pointed out the donor. Will, Mourdant, a very rich young man, loved Kate. He had suffered deeply when she refused his proffered hand, and it made him sorrowful at heart to hear that she loved Richard Brace instead of him. But now that poor Richard was dead, Will's hopes were once more awakened, and he resolved to make Kate his wife. It was not long before he began to visit the cottage, and escort Kate to church. He renewed his sighs of love, and all in such a quiet way that there was no avoiding him. Then neighbors began to whisper among themselves, and to give Kate what *they* considered good advice. Even her old grandmother said, softly—

"Will Mourdant is a fine young man, and grieving for poor Dick will never bring him back to life again."

Will, confident of his success, came oftener and was still more devoted. One night Kate bent over her work, stitching and thinking, thinking and stitching, oh, how wearily! when her old grandmother said,

"Kate, you had better marry Will Mourdant. He wants you, and poor Dick is dead."

She had never spoken so plainly before, and Kate dropped her work and looked up a moment in silence, and then, burying her face in her hands, she burst into a flood of bitter tears.

"Oh, dear! Granny," she sobbed, "they *all* say *that* to me. Don't *you* be as cruel as the rest are—pray do not."

"I am not cruel, but kind. You are killing yourself by this hard work, any one can see that. I am very old, and when I am dead there will be no one on earth to care for you."

"Then I shall soon die," too,. sobbed Kate, and come to meet you in heaven."

There were no selfish thoughts in her grandmother's bosom, but she knew it was the only way to gain Kate over to what she believed to be the best.

"For my part, I expect to die in the Poorhouse, or starve," she continued.

"Oh! Grandmother!" cried Kate.

"Yes. If you fall sick, or are out of work, that is what I may *expect.* If you marry Will, I may yet end my days in comfort. But it is better as it is, if you would be unhappy with him."

Starvation! the poorhouse! for her dear old grandmother! Kate could not bear the thought.

That night, after her old grandmother had gone to bed, Kate sat up weeping over the fading embers of the fire. Bye and bye she took the candle, and stood before the mirror. She saw her thin features, and the hectic flush in her cheeks, and felt a quick flutter of her heart.

"They are right," she sighed, "I cannot live long, and I should leave poor Granny to starve. If my little span of life will buy comfort for her, it shall be given. Yes, Will Mourdant, for her sake you shall have my hand, even though I cannot give you my broken heart."

As she spoke, the old clock on the mantel struck the hour of midnight, in slow, solemn strokes, as though it rang the knell of youth and love.

Before winter, Kate Raymond became the wife of Will Mourdant, and oh, how she regreted the act! Every day her regrets increased, until she began to loathe the very sight of her husband, and would shudder and shrink from his touch.

One night she was all alone. Her grandmother had gone to visit some friends, and her husband was absent in the city. She sat thinking that eternal thought of him now lost to her forever, when there came a sudden rap at the door. A strange voice said—

"Be not afraid, I am your friend!"

She opened the door and peered out. A tall man, wrapped in a cloak, with a slouch hat concealing his features, stood in the snow.

"I bring you a message," he continued, as he entered the house.

Kate mechanically offered him a chair, but could not speak.

"I am a sailor," began the stranger without removing his hat. "I left this place two years ago, in the ship Jenny Lind. There was a friend of yours on board. He was a friend of mine, also. His name was Richard Brace."

Kate could not speak, she only bowed her head and listened.

"We had a prosperous voyage," continued the stranger in the same husky voice, "and were homeward bound. But one morning the sun was hidden from us by black threatening clouds, and the dark horizon and white foaming waves, warned us of a storm. Soon our vessel was driven before the wind, a helpless wreck. Life was periled by remaining upon her longer, and the boats were soon filled by the crew and passengers. Some, God help them ! were left behind. There was no room for them in the boats. In our boat were the captain and his wife, four sailors ; Richard Brace and myself. I shall never forget the lady's despairing white face. Her great dark eyes were fastened on her husband, and she never turned them to any other object, not even on the babe at her breast. The child went first. We had drifted on three days, and our provisions were all gone, when it grew cold within its mother's arms ; and she would not unclasp them from its little form, but held it until by and by she quietly drooped upon her husband's breast, raised her lips to his, and breathed her last without a struggle. The captain loved her dearly. Two years of wedded life had made him only the fonder of his treasure. I think his heart was broken and his brain turned, for after sitting an hour with the corpse of his wife and of his child folded to him, he calmly dropped them over the side of the boat, saying, " Good bye !" He then, before we could guess his intentions, sprang into the sea after them, and in a moment the waves covered him from our sight. One by one, our four companions died at the oars. We had no hope of succor, but waited every moment for the ending of our misery. I stood up in the boat, to take my last view of the ocean, now calm and beautiful as though the storm had never been. I was too weak to use the oars, and the sky and sea swam before my eyes. "It is death," I said. "In an hour all will be over." But, as I spoke, I saw the white sails and dark hull of a vessel, far in the distance. I had given up all hope, but now I prayed aloud. I struggled with death, and fought against oblivion, and help came at last. We were soon on board a Spanish vessel, and rough hands nursed us kindly back to health."

"Richard! tell me of Richard!" cried Kate, seizing the stranger's arm. "Oh, why is he not here? Do tell why!"

The broad hat was thrown off, and the voice changed to its own clear tones, and Richard Brace himself, looked down into her face with his honest tear-filled eyes, and clasped her to his heart.

Oh! how joyful Kate was then. But when she grew calm, she remembered that *terrible truth.*

"My *husband!*" she gasped in frenzy. "He —*he* will return, perhaps to-night!" Consciousness forsook her, and she sank to the floor.

"Fly with me!" said Richard, pressing her warmly to him. "I know all—all—everything. Fly with me on the instant! Pause to arrange nothing! The next express train passes in half an hour, and we can reach the city to-night! Quick!—your bonnet and shawl!"

Delirious with excitement,—from joy at Richard's return to life, and fear that her husband would come,—Kate did not pause to think; and when Will Mourdant did return next day, he found his wife had flown. Full of rage, he started off in pursuit; and after hunting nearly a whole week, the fugitives were found at a city hotel, with their names registered as Mr. and Mrs. ——. A ludicrous scene ensued. There was a crash of furniture, harsh words and blows, but Richard Brace came off the victor. Then there was a warrant, and a hearing before a police justice, but Will Mourdant lost his wife.

Six months afterwards, Richard Brace was tired of Kate. Accepting an appointment of captain, and without saying even a cold fare well, he sailed on a voyage to the Pacific. Kate wept. She was frantic, and would have followed, but the wide, deep sea lay between them, and she could not even upbraid him for his cruelty. She could only weep.

Poor Kate! She had no friend left to console her. She was now really alone. Her grandmother lay in the grave, and her deserted husband cared never to see her again. In her despair, she swallowed poison ; but the dose was too large, and only made her sick, and all the more miserable. A month was quite sufficient to expend all her money, and then the hotel keeper notified her that he wished to have his rooms. Kate's trunks were piled up in the office hall, and she sat weeping in the public parlor. A stranger saw her distress, and begged to know what he could do to assist her. And now, for the *first* time in her life, she answered with a deliberate and wicked lie:

"I've been robbed. My portemonniae, with all my money, was cut from my pocket, and I have no friends in the city." She looked the picture of despair, and the stranger being rich, and fond of adventure, he was ready enough to console with a pretty woman. He inquired her history, and she deceived with false stories. Yet she only did what he was striving to do. Both wished to deceive. Business called him out, and he placed a hundred dollar bank bill in her hand, saying that he would soon return. The moment he was gone, she crushed the bill up tightly in her grasp, and rang the bell for a carriage. She walked up and down the parlor, and then in the hall, until the carriage should come. As she walked, her tears dried up, and she murmured to herself, "I will—I *will*—it is *now* my only chance!" The carriage was announced, and she took her leave.

* * * * * * *

Only five years have elapsed since Kate Raymond left that hotel, with the hundred dollar bill given her by that stranger. Only five years have come and gone since then. But where is she now? Echo answers, "She is *there!*" Kate Raymond's innocence and beauty have gone forever. Look at her portrait, and see how haggard and wan it is! A wretched outcast wife!

Oh, heavenly Father, in thy mercy, look down upon her with pity.

* * * * * * *

Will not the heart of many a wife beat quickly, as she reads the brief narrative here given of poor Kate Raymond? Oh, indeed it will! for in this vain world of strife for position, or perhaps for the plainest necessaries of existence, it often happens that love has been thrown aside for prospect of gain; and then when the fatal decision is made, the heart leadens and settles sadly down to wither and die, or recklessly bursts the bonds of matrimony, to riot in shame, and perish in sorrow. Beware, young woman, how you crush down the love that is now pleading in your heart, and choose gold instead thereof, for the chances are much against your happiness in the doubtful, and always uncertain future. Not even the holy bonds of wedlock can gladden a dejected heart, made lonely and desolate for the want of that love, which could have sustained it through weal or woe. Ah, and shudder at the possibility of forgetting the compact of society and law, after the first mistake is made, for then the voyage of life would be on a treacherous sea of painful calms and tempests of peril, with only the fragments of a wreck to float upon, and, perchance, with the certainty of eventual destruction on the rocks of despair.

The histories of other wives might be written to show the fate of the fallen, though it seldom happens that a trusting heart is so bitterly deceived by circumstances, or so cruelly forsaken by the object of its love and the being for whom good name and all has been bartered in haste. Yet, poor Kate's misfortune is another instance to prove the inconstancy of man towards a woman who sacrifices her self-respect. Indeed, respect is the pith of faithful love. Love will always bow to respect, and abides in only doubtful trust when respect has gone.

MRS. GRAMPUS.

MRS. GRAMPUS:

THE BOARDING-HOUSE KEEPER.

Offend her, and she knows not to forgive!
Oblige her, and she'll hate you while you live.—POPE.

RS. Grampus hates the world, but loves money, and derives a large profit from the income of an extensive boarding-house. Every now and then, a little bit of paper is pasted outside of her door, to notify passers by, that she can accommodate two single gentlemen, or a gentleman and wife, with a furnished back or front room, on the third or fourth floor. Sometimes she answers advertisements in the daily papers. No matter if she does not have the accommodations advertisers state they want, she can easily answer them, and they may come and see. Hundreds of people have been provoked in this way, by Mrs. Grampus. She has no fixed price for board or for rooms, preferring to deal separately with each customer, and get the most she can. Her house includes three large old-fashioned dwellings, in the lower part of the city, on a street west of Broadway, and she generally has about fifty boarders lodging therein, from the parlor floor up to the attic, who pay variously,—some as high as ten dollars, and others as low as two. Among them, are many down town clerks, and a number of journeymen. The "two dollar" boarders are poor girls, who work in the shops and factories, and who lodge three or four, and even five together, in the smallest, and most uncomfortable dormitories. They must have a home somewhere, and as they are mostly without relations and friends in the city, they see a very wretched life of it. With wages seldom more than three and half or four dollars, they have but little to spare, after paying out the two dollars for board ; and that board is always required in *advance* by Mrs. Grampus. We will relate an instance of her shrewdness, as it occurred a few years ago :—

A modest and delicate young woman, who gave her name as Lizzie, applied for a single room, and Mrs, Grampus hired her one of the back attics. She declined telling her history, and worked very hard day and night with her needle ; but at length her health gave out, and she fell sick. She had no friends, her money was all gone, and she sank rapidly. She had revealed only her *first* name, and stated that she came from the country, thinking she could find remunerative employment in the city. There might have been a sad mystery in her poor lonely heart, but that was sacred. She sat in her little chamber, and tears coursed down her pale cheeks. One evening the door opened and Mrs. Grampus entered. There was a heartless smile on her countenance. She looked Lizzie almost through, and then opened her mouth roughly.

Mrs. Grampus—Young woman, this is the third time I have told you to pay what you owe me, or to leave my house.

Lizzie—Oh, madam, I *will* pay you as soon I get well again. Indeed, I will pay you all.

Mrs. Grampus—*That* won't satisfy *me.* I've waited long enough. If you don't pay me this very night, I'll tumble you into the street.

Lizzie—Oh, do not turn me into the street, madam, I shall die there without shelter. I have no friends—no one to aid me. I have been sick so long—have given you dollar after dollar, from week to week, until all is gone. Oh, do let me remain a little longer. I shall soon be able to work again, and I will then toil without ceasing, until I have paid you every cent. Oh, madam, I am sick, I am very sick. Pity me, madam, I implore you!

MRS. GRAMPUS—Pity! Don't talk to *me* about pity Why should I pity you, eh, while you got a diamond ring on your finger—a *real* diamond? *Pity*, indeed! Give *me* that ring if you would have me let you remain: give *that* to me, and I'll convert it into *money*. A diamond ring, indeed, on *your* finger. Come, take it off.

LIZZIE—Surely you would not take *that*. It was the gift of my dear mother. It was given to her by my father in their early wedded days, and they are both dead now. Oh, I cannot part with *that*; ask for any thing else,—take all I have, even the clothes from my back, but not that ring!

MRS. GRAMPUS—Your *mother!* What care I *who* gave it to you? You owe *me* for board, and I will *sell* that to get my money.

Tears, entreaties, and prayers were of no avail. The ring was sold.

A few more weeks elapsed, and another corpse was carried to the grave. The history of poor Lizzie remained unknown, aud she was soon forgotten.

We will relate one other instance of Mrs. Grampus' kindness, and then leave her to go on working out her destiny.

There was a time when Mrs. Grampus had only the cheap garments on her back and the slender contents of a small trunk, which she could call her own, and she then had two little children. Her husband died early, and left her nothing but incumbrances and poverty. Like many other women on the verge of despair, she took to sewing, and tried to live in that way. It was hard struggling, but her children both died of a fever, and she was sadder and freer. By the assistance of one Mr. Jones, a good, kind man, who loaned her money, she was enabled to take a house and keep boarders. She had good luck, and did very well. In a few years, she took a larger house, and bought all the furniture for cash. Mrs. Grampus began to feel rich. But Mr. Jones was a boarder at her house until one slippery day in winter, he fell while crossing the track of the railroad in West Broadway, and before he could regain his feet, a car wheel passed over his limbs, nearly killing him on the spot. Two policemen took him home in a carriage. They rang the bell, and stood ready to enter with their bleeding burden. The door was opened, and the shrill voice of Mrs. Grampus cried out—

"Take him to the hospital,—he can't come in here with that nasty blood, to spoil *my* carpets!"

The policemen remonstrated, and the poor man groaned with agony, but she slammed the door in their faces, and they conveyed him to the hospital; but before they could arrive there, Mr. Jones was *dead!*

* * * * * * *

Not long ago, a reputed widow, who "keeps boarders" in Bank street, actually refused to permit one of her servants to summon a physician for a lady boarder, who was dying in her house. She entertained a spite towards the lady because, on a previous occasion, she had complained of the sour bread and bad butter. In her malice, she now forbade her servants stirring a single step after a physician. The lady was in great suffering; and fearful of instant death, she begged and implored, and freely offered money; but the heartless woman obstinately refused.

"Let her get a doctor herself, if she wants one. I'll not assist her."

"But she will die," interposed the chambermaid, who had seen the lady's distress.

"Well, that's no business of mine," retorted the fiend.

Fortunately, a friend called just in time to save the lady's life; and as soon as her health permitted, she vacated her rooms.

SALLIE MUNN.

SALLIE MUNN:

THE WIDOW'S DAUGHTER.

> But Satan now is wiser than of yore,
> And tempts by making rich, not making poor.—POPE.

MRS. Munn was a happy wife. She loved her husband, and was almost idolized by him in return. Sallie was their only child. Mr. Munn was not rich, but by industry and good habits, he managed to live well, until a sudden attack of disease took away his life. Then Mrs. Munn was left alone, in grief and sorrow, to struggle through her troubles and trials as best she might. The little left by her husband soon disappeared, and then her hands must earn money to provide for her wants and the wants of her child. She had married against the will of her relatives, and now they refused to aid her. But she was proud, and kept aloof from them, and tried to make the best of her lot.

A few years quickly past away, and almost before she could realize the fact, her daughter was sixteen. It was now time that she should do something to help her mother in providing for their living. She read the " Wants " in the daily papers, and bye and bye she found a situation in a Broadway refreshment saloon. There, she was an object of particular interest to the gentlemen, who frequently patronized the place on purpose to exchange a few words with her. Many were the allurements that came in still whispers to her youthful ear, but thanks to the good principles taught and strengthened by the example and precepts of her dear mother, she schooled herself to hear, and to only laugh or smile replies, and not to harbor, for an instant, any thought of doing wrong. When she sometimes caught herself pondering over the dazzling pictures drawn by her tempters, she would blush, and banish them from her mind.

One evening, a lady and gentleman entered the saloon for refreshments, and it happened that Sallie waited on them. As she did so, she was annoyed by the steady gaze of the gentleman. She tried to avoid it, but could not. Even the lady accompanying the gentleman observed him, and remarked, in an undertone,

"You seem particularly struck."

"So I am. You know I am a great admirer of pretty women," smiled the gentleman.

The lady returned his smile, and jestingly said—

"What would your wife say, if she were here to witness your admiration? You know she is inclined to jealousy."

With a cold curl of his lip, he leaned over towards her, and asked—

"What would *you* say if she were here?"

A crimson flush was the only response she made. No other words passed between them before they finished their wine and left. As they withdrew, the gentleman slipped a card into Sallie's hand, on which was hastily written with a pencil, unseen by the lady—

"*Unexpectedly, in me you will find a valuable friend. We shall meet again.*"

Sallie read the card, and then tore it into pieces with contempt, mentally ejaculating—

"What presumption he has, to be sure! These men seem to think that I am here for no other purpose but to fall in love with them. Fools!"

But Sallie could not help thinking about the gentleman, and repeating over to herself the words written on the card. She went to bed that night with a sadness quite unusual for her to feel, and her first thought in the morning was of that gentleman and his card.

" Pshaw !" she reasoned to herself, " it is absurd and ridiculous. How dare he take such a liberty ! I'll not think of him any more—not I !"

Oh ! woman's heart is a riddle. The very thing she resolves not to think of, is sure to be uppermost in her mind. She declares that she will *not*, and is all the while acting contrary to her declarations.

The gentleman entered the saloon the next evening, and her heart fluttered and her cheeks were like fire. He passed her with a respectful bow and a pleasant smile. She did not offer to wait on him, and he beckoned her to him.

" I'll not come," she muttered. " No, indeed ! There are enough besides me to wait on him. I'll not come !" And yet, even as she was thus muttering, she went to him, and received his order. She dared not raise her eyes, for she felt his gaze upon her.

He did not remain long, and said nothing to her except what pertained to the refreshment he required. When he was gone, she saw a diminutive box lying on the table, but she would not touch it.

" It may lie there, for all I care," she thought. " If he can't take care of his things. he deserves to lose them."

She walked off, and even her woman's curiosity did not compel her to examine what it might be. Presently, one of the other attendant's saw the box, and took it up.

"Put that down!" cried Sallie, rushing up to the table, "I'll take care of it for him. You needn't trouble yourself, Miss P——"

How quickly changed! A moment before she refused to touch it, and now she would have taken it by force.

"Oh, I see!" said Miss P——, laughing and attracting the attention of the other girls. "He is a rich lover of yours—eh? There it is; take it. Your name is written on the cover."

Sallie seized the tiny thing, and read on the outside—"*Presented to Miss Sallie Munn.*" She trembled, and put it it her bosom. Her comrades all laughed and giggled, and looked askance, and winked, and made impertinent signs.

As soon as she had left the saloon to go home, Sallie tore open the box, and it contained a magnificent cluster of diamonds, set in a ring. To it was fastened a little slip of paper with these words upon it—"*Keep this, and I will add to it a thousand times its value.*"

* * * * *

We cannot relate all that followed. Our pages are limited, and we must make Sallie's story a short one.

The gentleman continued his visits, and added present to present, until Sallie had actually learned to love him. We say love—but perhaps it was infatuation. At least, it was a fatal spell that had cast itself about her heart. Marriage was not *his* purpose, though it was hers. He was carrying out a deep-laid plan for her ruin ; but on the day and almost the very hour which would have completed her ruin, he was taken charge of by the criminal law. Next day, the arrest of a noted forger, and many startling disclosures connected with his crimes, were published in all the newspapers. That forger was Sallie's rich lover. A few months afterwards, he went to State Prison, where he still remains, serving out a sentence of ten years.

And yet, Sallie will not listen to his guilt. She says he is innocent, and mourns the very event which saved her in the moment of her greatest peril. Her mother often remonstrates with her, but she persists in clinging to the hope of meeting him again when his captivity expires.

"You know he has a wife and several children, who were left destitute by his incarceration in prison," says her mother, sharply.

"But she is not his *lawful* wife," replies Sallie. "He told me he was *not* married, and I believe him."

Ah! Sallie will think differently when she is ten years older.

NANCY SCROGGS.

NANCY SCROGGS:

THE LAGER BEER WOMAN.

To what gulfs
A single deviation from the track of human duties leads.
—BYRON.

OHN Scroggs, an honest farmer in the eastern part of Connecticut, at the age twenty-four, married a widow of a gay turn and rather unsteady disposition. Scroggs never thought of inquiring into her history until he had made her his lawful wife. Better for him if he had inquired, but, good soul, he was then too much infatuated with her charms to give himself the least uneasiness about her worth and merits as a wife. She did not voluntarily let him into any of her secrets, and the marriage was duly consummated.

Unfortunate Scroggs! The honeymoon was soon over. One day, a strange man, with a green patch over his eye, inquired the way to Scroggs' farm. The man asked to see Mr.

Scroggs's wife, and, as a natural consequence, there was no little concern on Scroggs' mind as to what he wanted. A few minutes sufficed to elucidate the matter. The stranger entered the house, and clutching Mrs. Scroggs by the arm, he spoke in this wise :—

So, so ! I've found you, at last ! When I go off to Pike's Peak to dig gold and make a fortune for you, this is the way you do—eh ? A good wife, you are !"

Mrs. Scroggs screamed, and farmer Scroggs stood by, aghast. What could he say or do ? He was completely dumbfounded until Mrs. Scroggs' tongue began to move—

"I'm no wife of your'n, and I want you to take your hands off my arm. I'm the lawful wife of Mr. John Scroggs, and shall not allow you or any other feller to insult me !"

At this, Scroggs roused himself, and doubling his right fist, he threatened to strike the stranger in the face. He seemed to aim exactly at the eye covered with the green patch.

"I say ! look a-here, mister ! Gol darn if I ken stand it any longer !" he exclaimed in fury. He caught the stranger's coat collar in his left hand, so as to have a better chance to hit the covered eye, and went on—"That woman's mine ; I married her before Squire Engles, and, by thunder ! I ain't a-going to have her mauled round by you, or any other blasted straggler! You won't let go, *won't* you? Then, take *that!* and THAT!!"

John Scroggs weighed just two hundred and and forty pounds, and had muscle that might have terrified a prize-fighter, and his fist was doubly as large and thrice as hard as the fists of ordinary men. The stranger tumbled to the floor, and the blood ran from his bruised features. The battle was fought and won. John Scroggs felt, for all the world, like a hero.

Before the sun set that evening, the stranger had departed from the Scroggs' mansion. But alas, for Scroggs! His peace had been invaded, and now he grew distrustful, and began to imagine all sorts of things against his wife. From suspicions, he took to abusive language, and soon he and his wife were quarrelling, morning, noon, and night. Scroggs became very unhappy, and spent much of his time at the village tavern, only half a mile off. Matters grew worse every day. Words were not harsh enough, and then he introduced blows to keep the excitement up.

Blows from a man like John Scroggs would soon annihilate a giant; and being unable to defend herself, Mrs. Scroggs concluded to gather up what valuables she could carry, and fly to the city.

It was a cold December day, and the snow and rain made it very disagreeable out, for even the most rugged traveler, yet Mrs. Scroggs walked all the way to New Haven, in time for the night boat. Next morning she reached the city.

Poor Scroggs! Excessive drinking, and trouble of mind, made short work of his life. In less than three months after his wife left him, he died in a drunken fit.

There was a lawsuit between Mr. Scroggs' two brothers and Mrs. Scroggs, as to who should have the property. The case was about to be decided very much in favor of the brothers, when Mrs. Scroggs produced an heir. She came into court with an infant, and conclusively proved that John Scroggs deceased, was its father.

Mrs. Scroggs obtained possession of John Scroggs' estate. She was now quite rich. A lawyer helped her to sell the farm, and whatever else she was allowed.

With twelve thousand dollars in money, and a rather pretty face for one of her class, she was not long in finding an opening in the way of business. A traveling showman proposed to establish a Free Concert Saloon, in the city, He advertised for a female partner, with some little capital. Among the answers he received, there was one which read thus :—

I have abundant means for embarking in the enterprise alluded to by the advertiser, and would like an interview. I may be seen at the Smithsonian Hotel, any hour in the forenoon, to-morrow or next day. NANCY SCROGGS.

The interview took place, and Nancy Scroggs became the monied partner in a new saloon, devoted to free concerts and lager beer. There was no lack of custom, but in some way unknown to Nancy, the expenses of the concern always came out more than the receipts at the bar. More money was wanted every now and then ; and to top all, there was an execution issued against the place, to satisfy a large judgment obtained against her without her knowledge, by one Johnson, Jones, or Brown. The lease, good will, and fixtures, were sold ; and to make up the whole amount, her bank account was also seriously disturbed. She raved and vowed revenge, but she had fallen into the hands of sharpers, and there was no hope for her. But the partnership was dissolved.

In exactly one year after the death of John Scroggs, his widow Nancy parted with the last dollar of his estate. And will the reader believe it, she then proposed to return and live with her first husband : that man who was so roughly used by John Scroggs, when he visited the farm house out in Connecticut. That individual declined any renewal of past associations, and she finally turned herself to account, by entering into the service of a Dutchman in the lager bier business ; sometimes acting as waiteress, and at others, as partner in a quiet game of cards with verdant young men from the West or the South.

The gentleman who gave us her portrait, and furnished these facts of her history, assures us that the likeness is remarkably correct, he having drawn it as she sat at the card-table with a country friend of his, to whom he was showing the "ins and outs" of the city.

* * * * * * * *

We need not say anything about the destiny of Nancy Scroggs, as her course is along the old track, trodden by so many who are vile. The hospital or the prison, will end her earthly career, and then her remains must be cast into potter's field.

SUSAN BRADLEY.

SUSAN BRADLEY:

THE CLERGYMAN'S WIFE.

Heaven but tries our virtue by affliction—
As oft the cloud that wraps the present hour
Serves but to lighten all our future days.—Byron.

AT the age of sixteen, Susan Bradley's mother went blind, and she began the serious task of earning a living by school-teaching. It was somewhat difficult to get an appointment; but through the aid of a retired butcher, who was a director, she obtained a place in one of the public schools. For his services, the director fancied that she ought to, ever after, look upon him as her patron benefactor. He further desired that she should fall in love with him, and adore him as her idol. But Susan's taste soared a little higher. She said to herself—

"He's all very well to have for a friend.

He's rich, and has influence ; but, dear me! I cannot think of him in any other relation."

One evening, she received a note from the director. It had evidently been written with much care, though so shockingly done that she could scarcely decypher it, at all. After poring over it perhaps half an hour, she translated its scrawls into these words :—

Mi deer Susan. You kno how long i been liking you and i kant be put oph any longer i neednt tell you as how that i ken make you as rich as i pleese, or i ken have you turned out of the schule in disgrace say the word and i will make one of my tennants muve out of the yallar kottage in arlinyton Row and set you up in there in grand stile—i have wated long anuff and now insist on your answer wether i am to be your devoted lovver or your ded ennemy. Jake who brings this, will wate fur your finel desisun. yourn as ever P——.

Susan Bradley was not to be frightened, nor was she to be bought, in that way.

"Ugh!" she sneered. "Such a letter from a school director! So, he's waited long enough, has he? and must have my final answer—eh? I'll let him see what I am made of! Oh! I could scratch his eyes out—that I could!" Then she tore off the fly-leaf of the director's letter, and wrote, in a large, bold hand, thus :

Sir :—You here have my final answer. For the hundredth and the last time, I repeat, No!

She did not even sign her name, but sealed it and gave it to the messenger.

The next day, Susan Bradley had a notice from the principal of the school, that her presence would be required no longer. She was expelled, and at the bottom of the note, there was a short postscript, which said :—

"It pains me to learn such evil reports. I had the greatest confidence in your moral worth, and I am extremely sorry that the evidences are so conclusively against your character."

Susan had a blind mother to maintain, and it was a great misfortune to be thus thrown out of a situation, in the dead of winter. Yet the cruelest part of her misery, was the insinuations written by the principal. She went to him and demanded an explanation, and, with tears, implored him to give her a chance for defence ; but he was in the pay of *his* master, the director, and she found no mercy in him.

With a heavy heart, she sought employment elsewhere. In the other schools, they were already full, and there seemed to be no hope for her. She tried a long time to get anything to do, that might support herself and her mother ; but whenever she was just on the point of getting a situation, a cold, distrustful look, would accompany a blunt refusal. The emissaries of the revengeful director, dogged her steps every day, and whispered falsehoods against her, into the ears of all who were inclined to employ her.

* * * * *

Susan Bradley and her mother were reduced to the verge of starvation; and when the cold snow blew in through the broken window-pane, and the last ember of fire died out in the old stove, there was a deep sigh to disturb the stillness of the room.

"Oh, mother! what shall we do?" sobbed Susan, burying her face in her mother's lap. "We have no more coal, and not a morsel of bread. Shall we perish here, in this dismal place? You cannot see, but it is growing dark, and the night will be very long."

"It is, indeed hard," replied her mother, in a tremulous tone, but we must put our trust in God. He *only* can help us now!"

"I beg your pardon, Mrs. Bradley," said a man's voice, "*I* have come to help you!"

Susan and her mother started in surprise, not dreaming that any one was near.

"You here!" exclaimed Susan, springing to her feet, as her eyes rested upon the form and face of her enemy, the director, who had entered by stealth. "You come to help us—*you?*"

"Even so," smiled the director, offering his hand. "I heard that you were in trouble, and throwing aside my bitter feelings of the past,

I now come to offer you whatever assistance I can give."

Susan shrank from his proffered hand, and she and her mother both bade him depart.

"We will sooner starve!" said the mother.

"Aye," coincided Susan, putting her arm around her parent's neck, "we will perish here with hunger and cold, rather than accept any bounty from you."

"How?" exclaimed the director, knitting his brows in anger. "Do you treat my offer with a refusal? You have already felt my wrath—be careful how you enrage me again. I have come now with a peace offering. Refuse it, and I'll haunt you into the grave!"

"We do refuse! Your persecutions have brought us to our present condition; but you can harm us no more." Susan spoke fearlessly. "We can but starve; and therefore we defy you!"

"Miss Bradley," said the director, "you have sealed your fate." He approached the door, and, as there was no key, he slipped the bolt.

"What are you doing, sir?" cried Susan, in alarm.

"You shall see!" was the director's answer, as he drew the window-blind. "You shall see!"

A loud scream from Susan echoed out in the hall, and, almost in the same instant, there were quick knocks against the door. Susan gave another scream, crying "Help!—who's there?'

"A friend," was the answer from without.

Susan sprang up to remove the bolt. The director endeavored to restrain her, but she eluded his grasp, and, in a twinkle, the door was wide open.

"How is this?" exclaimed the new comer, looking at the director, in surprise.

Susan ventured to say—"That man is a monster! Pray, shield us from him."

"He a monster!" ejaculated the new comer, "why, I know him well. He is a member of my church, and a wealthy man!"

* * * * *

Susan Bradley's life was brighter and brighter from that hour. The new comer was the charitable clergyman of a neighboring church. By chance, he had heard of the destitution of Mrs. Bradley and Susan, and had sought out their abode to render them aid. He arrived just in time.

Being a widower, the clergyman conceived a love for Susan, and it was not long before he made her his wife. She is now the happy mother of two girls and a boy. Her blind mother still lives, and although she cannot see the faces of her grandchildren, she loves them dearly, and often sits rocking them all in her lap together, by the hour.

The school director is not a member of the clergyman's church, now. He is dead.

STELLA RISDON.

STELLA RISDON:

THE OLD MAN'S DARLING.

"If she will, she will—you may depend on't,
And if she won't, she won't—so there's an end on't."

AVID Risdon began life a poor boy. Hard work and many long years of steady perseverance, made him a fortune. From poverty, he ascended to great wealth. He married early, but his wife died in child-birth, and left him a motherless babe. He was a very avaricious man, and the world said he had no heart or feeling for any thing but himself and money. Yet the world does not always know every thing, for David Risdon loved his child as tenderly as a father could love. He never married again. His affections, that were not buried with his dead wife, were centered in his living daughter, who matured into a beautiful woman. She was sought after by many men who stood ready to become her husband, and she soon made a choice.

Like her mother, she died in child-birth too. They put her away in her grave, and her babe began existence just as she had before it, in the dawn of her own life. David Risdon nearly lost his reason, the blow was so hard for him to bear ; but as he had done twenty years ago, he tried to do now. He grieved for the mother, and strove to cherish the offspring. A grand-daughter occupied the place in his heart, where daughter and wife had been nestled, each in turn, long before. A few years changed the babe into a romping girl, with long curls and ribbons. The old man almost forgot his wife and his daughter, because his young darling, now dancing about his arm chair, was to him a living embodiment of them all. Her features were exactly her mother's and grandmother's, so were her voice, her gait, and her manner ; and her very laughter, which rang so loudly through the halls of his mansion, was the clear silvery music, he had heard twenty and forty years ago. He would often put his withered arms round her slender waist, and draw her to him, as he sat in his easy chair, and she would kiss his wrinkled cheeks, and pale, blue-veined brow, with her red warm lips ; her flaxen curls would mingle with his snowy locks, and he would doatingly murmur—

"Does Stilla love her old grandpa?"

And then she, with arch coquetry, would answer—

"Does grandpa love his Stella?"

Sometimes she would sit on a stool near him, while he told her about her grandmother and her mother, how they had each died, how exactly alike they were, and how he had loved them, and how only she now remained.

And who knows but what I too shall die in the same way?" said Stella one time, when the old man was telling her the oft told story. She looked up into his face seriously, and two large tears rolled down his cheeks. His heart was very full just then, and she wiped the ugly tears away, and kissed the spots she wiped them from.

At length, Stella did become a wife; and to please the old man, her husband consented that they should remain and live in the mansion. Old age had left little but gray hairs and dry bones, and ere long the debt of nature must be paid.

Stella loved her husband, but she had been spoiled by the extreme indulgence of her grandpa, and it was only a few months before she quarreled with him, and they then pouted for a whole week. A reconciliation smoothed matters over for a little while, but soon the estrangement was greater than ever. Stella would fly to the arms of grandpa, and pour out all her grievances, and he took her part, and said harsh things to her husband. Bad became worse, until upon one particular occasion, her conduct was so very provoking, that her husband could not keep down his temper, and Stella only exasperated him all the more by tantalizing words. He forget himself, and sprang towards her to commit violence. She flew to the arms of her grandpa, and a blow intended for her, leveled the old man to the floor. Terrified and ashamed of what he had done, the husband raised him up, and by expressions of regret, begged for pardon. It was a frail old bark, and its last voyage nearly run.

That blow was death!

Old David Risdon lived only a week longer. He died, and was buried in Greenwood, beside the graves of his wife and daughter.

A will made Stella sole heir to her grandpa's wealth. She and her husband did not exchange a word even at the funeral, and when the sad rites were over, they separated forever. Stella was rich, and plunged wildly into dissipation. The gentle girl and young wife, was transformed into quite another being. Three years after her dissipation began, she scarcely had a home.

Not long ago, the report of a pistol alarmed the inmates of a boarding house, in the upper part of the city. They rushed to the apartment the sound came from, and there on the floor lay Stella Risdon. A pistol was near her, and the blood flowed thick and fast from a wound in her left temple.

The newspapers contained a long paragraph, on the "Attempted suicide of a fast young woman."

Stella Risdon recovered, and is living we know not where nor how. But she denies attempting to destroy her life, and says that the pistol was in the hands of a would-be assassin. She does not say who it was, but some have strongly hinted that it might have been her deserted husband. By looking at her picture, the reader will perceive how she conceals the disfiguring scar left from the wound in her temple. She dresses her hair, so that a few truant tresses seem carelessly to fall over the spot. She is still young and pretty, and may live many years. But her future must be precarious indeed. If she has any remnants of a heart left, it may yet ache and torture her badly enough before she dies.

* * * * * * *

When we reflect how erroneous the great majority of daughters, and grand-daughters are now educated, it does not seem strange that there should be quarrels and troubles between them and their husbands in future life. While girls are reared with the sole object of catching rich men, and securing "excellent matches," we can not wonder if they are totally unfitted to become wives. They may not be petted and spoiled like Stella Risdon, but their notion of matrimonial existence is often confined to getting husbands, without having learned the first art of keeping them. Men who are attracted by pretty faces, or by any charm, whether of body or mind, naturally expect the attraction to continue after the ceremony is performed. Girls who know how to catch, should also know the art of keeping. Herein lies one of the greatest secrets of unhappiness in married life. Lovers who are all sweetness and consideration before marriage, in nine cases out of ten, drop "such little nonsense," as they then call it, after going through a very brief honey-moon, and of course begin to feel dissatisfied with each other. If marriage was only for a day, a week, or a month, or we will say even a year, then it might do to study the witchery of attraction, without the magic art of keeping. But, dear girls, marriage is for life. Look, then, to that life, before the opportunity is lost forever.

CLARA COLLIER.

CLARA COLLIER:

THE DISOWNED.

> "The greatest attribute of heaven is mercy,
> And 'tis the crown of justice, and the glory,
> Where it may kill with right, to save with pity."

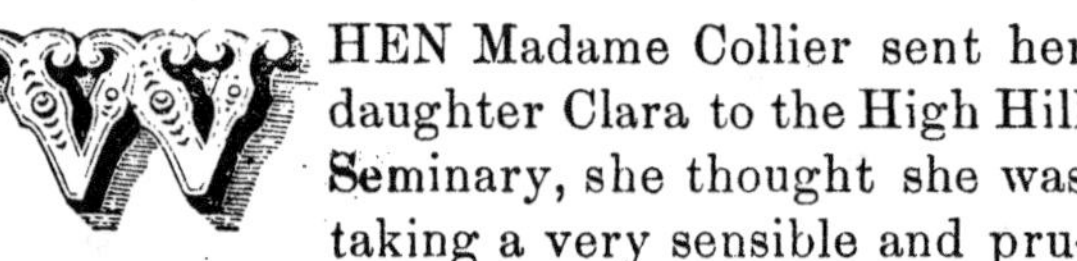

WHEN Madame Collier sent her daughter Clara to the High Hill Seminary, she thought she was taking a very sensible and prudent step towards perfecting her education and preserving her morals pure. Madame had never been to a seminary herself, as a pupil, though she knew many ladies who had been taught in them, and two or three proprietors.

Clara was fourteen, and began to fancy that she was quite a lady. Her mother, fully as sensible as the average of city mothers, foresaw that unless she sent her away from home, and put her under the most rigid restraint, there would soon be an end of her studies.

" And, bless you," said Madame to her husband, " it's just the place for girls."

" It may be," replied her husband, with an incredulous shrug of his shoulders, " but I have no time to ascertain. Business demands my attention down town. You may do as you please."

" Certainly, I shall do as I please!" said Madame, when her husband was out of hearing.

Clara cried, and made frantic objections to going to High Hill, but Madame was resolute.

It required only a month or so to banish the gloom from Clara's mind. Her home was soon completely forgotten. The daily routine of school, and the little excitements of the pupils, kept her from the least approach to melancholy.

" *Clara's conduct is excellent*," wrote the lady principal, home to her mother. " *We look upon her as the example of her class.*"

Meanwhile, Madame Collier and her husband gave themselves no uneasiness about their daughter, and went on in their fashionable way.

Bye and bye, the principal wrote again :—

" *It is my painful duty to inform you that your daughter, Clara, has disappeared from High Hill, and is nowhere to be found. See has eloped with a married man!*"

There was a great excitement in the house

of Collier when that letter came. Madame flew about like one possessed, and her husband swore at seminaries in general.

"Here we are, disgraced forever, by that good for nothing jade!" raved Madame.

"And that's what comes of sending her to High Hill!" growled Collier. "And now, the next thing is to find her, and bring her home."

"What!" cried Madame, "bring her back, and be sneered at by the whole city, every time she goes into sight? No! Mr. Collier. Clara shall never enter my house again. She has forfeited all claims to *my* love or affection, and I disown her—Mr. Collier, I disown her!"

"Ugh! you disown her, do you?" responded Collier.

"I do—she shall never enter *my* house again."

"She shall never enter *your* house? Pray, *where* is your house, madame?"

"Where? why, *here*—here, sir!" Madame emphasized her words strongly.

"And you refuse to let her return here to your house?"

"Mr. Collier, you have my decision." Madame swept out of the room, and left her husband standing by the window, biting his lip in the depths of thought. Presently, he strode out of the room himself, and hastily left the house.

That day and the next, were spent by Collier in writing letters and sending messengers in all directions, in search of his runaway daughter. A week elapsed, and a letter came. Collier knew the handwriting, and trembled as he broke the seal:—

DEAR PA:—*If I come home, will you forgive me?* CLARA.

He glanced at the post-mark, and was off in the first conveyance to Boston, where he found Clara, in great distress, and looking very haggard and sick from crying and mental suffering. He asked her but few questions. She related how she had been deceived by a married man, a music teacher at the seminary, and found out the deception only when the man's wife traced them up, and confronted him in her presence, and abused her in a violent manner. She was now sorry enough for what she had done, and wanted to go home. Collier reasoned within himself that, under the circumstances, it would be better to let the man go unpunished, than to give the matter publicity. He thought it would be much better to keep the matter profoundly a secret, if he possibly could.

"There is yet some hope," he said to himself; and, taking Clara in his arms, he kissed her. "Poor child!" he mourned aloud, "you shall go home, and we will forget it all."

Collier entered his own house, with his own daughter, and said to his wife, the mother of that daughter—

"Here is Clara. Pray, forgive her, as I have done."

Clara stood ready to fly into her mother's arms. Her eyes were full of tears, and her heart beat quickly.

"Dear mother!" she cried, and started towards her.

"Don't come near me!" exclaimed Madame, with a harsh, cold sneer. "Go to the arms of your married lover—you can't remain here!"

There was a painful scene in the house of Collier that night, and the next day Clara was removed by her father to lodgings elsewhere. Had he persisted in keeping her in his house, against the opposition of her mother, he feared the whole affair would be made public before the quarrel was ended; so he decided to take a quiet course, until the mother might listen to reason and human feeling. But her heart was devoted to the opinion of the world, and no influence could change her resolution.

* * * * *

Clara Collier's father died, and she had no protector. Some malicious tongue whispered it about how she had been deluded at High Hill, and then a hundred bitter remarks were uttered by her acquaintances. And then, everybody saw into the strangeness of her having lived apart from her mother.

Clara was not poor, but had the wealth left by her father been a thousand times greater, it could not have shielded her from this blast of slander. She was engaged to a wealthy gentleman, and would have become an honorable wife, but the poison of scandal reached the ear of her intended, and he left her.

* * * * *

Fifteen years have passed, and Clara Collier has long been known to all the fast men of the city. Her house is said to be a palace of art and luxury. Her mother is dead, but she has numerous relatives living, and when her name is spoken in the hearing of any of them, they are offended, and look very solemn.

MRS GILBERT.

MARY GILBERT:

THE LADY OF FORTUNE.

"Fate is above us all;
We struggle, but what matters our endeavor?
Our doom is gone beyond our own recall!
May we deny or mitigate it? NEVER!"

IN looking at the portrait of Mary Gilbert, none would ever dream that she was once a ragged and bare-footed child of poverty. There is nothing in her face to lead even the cleverest physiognomist to draw such a conclusion; yet, thirty years ago, those very features were often dirt-stained and moist with tears, forced by hunger and cold.

About the year 1831, a European lady came to New York, and remained here only a few months, during which time she gave birth to a female child. As soon as she was able, she prepared to recross the ocean for her home. She did not take her babe with her. She placed it in the care of a poor widow woman, then living in the eastern part of the city. Leaving a good supply of money with the widow, to reward her for the best care of the child, its mother departed, with promises to send more money every six months. It was also arranged that the widow should correspond with the lady as often as practicable, with full tidings of the child.

But, alas! for the uncertainty of all earthly things. The ship in which the lady sailed, was wrecked off the coast of Ireland, in a terrible storm, and it was said that all on board were drowned.

Six months went by, and no remittance came to the widow, as it was promised. She did not know of the loss of the ship, and said to herself—

"The mother has forsaken her child, and left it a burden on me. I am poor, and must have bread."

So she took the child out in her arms, and sat down on a stoop in a street where wealthy people lived. She held out her hand, and, of those who passed to and fro, a few dropped either pennies or silver. Meeting with success, she continued doing the same thing every day, and, in a little while, she had plenty of money.

When the child was about five years old, a shrewd junk-shop dealer offered to buy her of the widow. This man made considerable money, by receiving and selling anything and everything that small children could pick up and steal. His offer was too tempting for the widow, and she gave the child over to him. The junk-shop keeper's wife then named her Mary. She was quick and bright, and soon learned to be very expert in the execution of little thefts. But, fortunately for her, the junk-shop keeper was suspected by the police, and finding that he would soon be arrested, he fled from the city, leaving his wife, and several vagabond children, to be taken charge of by the authorities, who sent them all to the House of Correction, where Mary remained, until one day a lady and gentleman, who were visiting the institution, took a liking to her face, and asked permission to remove her to their dwelling. They were wealthy people, and had no difficulty in getting possession of her. They put her to school, and, in the course of time, she became a very pretty and highly accomplished lady. Her benefactors had no children of their own, and they made much of her. The world, generally, thought that she was their own daughter.

At length, her adopted mother died, and,

after a proper interim of mourning, she was surprised to hear her adopted father ask her to become his second wife.

" You are only jesting," said Mary, who had been so long accustomed to call him father, and to look upon him with a reverence and respect, quite different from what she imagined she should feel for a husband.

"Far from a jest, I assure you," he replied. " There is no other being on earth for whom I have any love, while, to you, all the best sympathies of my heart are inclined. From the hour I first saw you, a poor child of sorrow, in the house of correction, my affection for you has been gradually increasing."

" Mary's eyes filled with tears when he spoke of what and where she was when he found her, and he kissed her, saying—" I did not wish to make you sad. I alluded to the past only to show how long you have been twining yourself around my heart."

" But what will be said of you, for marrying your adopted daughter?" asked Mary. " Will not the tongues of mischief begin to talk and tattle?"

" Let them talk. Their tattling cannot harm us."

* * * * * * *

There was a grand wedding at the house of

Simeon Gilbert, the rich stock jobber, and Mary, his adopted child, became his wife. There was a great talk about it, and many remarks and surmises were uttered.

"It is scarcely credible!" sneered a lady, who had intended to become Mr. Gilbert's second wife herself, if it could be brought about. "They always called her their daughter. Why! Mrs. Gilbert said, in my hearing, more than once, that Mary was their *only* child, and I'm sure that she would never have made so much of her if she had been merely *adopted!*"

"Yes, but the worst of all is her *origin*," interposed one Mrs. Fling. "Nobody ever knew it until she told it herself, and only the other day, to Mrs. Sneak, who seems to have taken an unaccountable interest in her since the wedding. Why, she told her, that before she was put in the House of Correction, she and half a dozen other little ragamuffins, earned their living by stealing for a junk-shop keeper!"

"What's that?" demanded Mr. Fling, suddenly roused from reading a morning paper, by hearing his wife mention certain words. "Who are you talking about, Mrs. Fling?"

Mrs. Fling explained, and Mr. Fling was thrown into a deep study. Presently a carriage drew up before the door.

"Madame Gilbert," announced the servant, throwing open the drawing-room doors.

"Oh! I'm so delighted! And how charming you are looking to-day!" smiled Mrs. Fling.

There was much kissing, and fussing, and many false declarations.

"You are not acquainted with my husband, I believe," said Mrs. Fling. "Allow me to present him."

Mr. Fling seemed embarrassed, but tried to show no signs of discomfiture. He was just in the act of executing one of his best postures of salutation, when Mrs. Gilbert turned pale, and gave a terrible scream. Mrs. Fling did not understand it, and was much dismayed. But Mr. Fling gave an imploring glance to Mrs. Gilbert, when she had recovered enough to raise her eyes, and that glance saved Mr. Fling from premature disgrace.

* * * * * * *

When Mrs. Gilbert sat alone with Mr. Gilbert the following evening, she asked him if he knew the husband of Mrs. Fling. Her name had been on their list of visitors some time, but his had not.

"I do not," he replied. "Why do you ask?"

"I'll tell you directly. How long has he lived in New York?"

"But a few years, I am told. They came

from Canada. Mr. Fling made a fortune in Montreal. He goes out very little, but his wife is present at all the fashionable gatherings."

"Well, Mr. Fling is the junk-shop keeper to whom I was indebted for my exploits in street vagrancy, and by which I got into the institution where you found me."

"Good heavens!" ejaculated Mr. Gilbert, "what strange things do happen!"

* * * * *

In a few days, Mr. Gilbert had learned a gread deal more about the Flings, and brought the news to Mary.

"I've made inquiries of every body who know any thing about them. Of Mr. Fling I can ascertain only what I told you the other evening, but I discovered that his wife was the daughter of an English gentleman of fortune. In consequence of the irregularities of her early life, she incurred the eternal·displeasure of her father, who sent her off to Canada on an annuity. She there fell in with Mr. Fling and became his wife."

While Mr. Gilbert was talking, a servant brought him a letter. He read it aloud :—

DEAR SIR,—*Since you excited my curiosity about the pedigree of the Flings, I have learned that before Mrs. Fling was finally banished by her father, she had been sent to this city, to hide the evidences of her improper conduct with a wild young nobleman. She left the child here, in care of one Mrs. Done, and returned in a ship which was wrecked on the voyage. All on board perished, with the exception of three. She was one of the saved. But from some interception, she was unable to keep up a correspondence with widow Done, and in time she almost forgot she had ever been a mother."*

"My mother!" exclaimed Mary, snatching the letter from Mr. Gilbert's hands, before he had finished. "My mother! The mystery of my life is now explained. Mr. Fling can assist me in making the charge complete. I will go this instant and see him."

"A visitor is below," said the servant, presenting a card. "He desires to see Mrs. Gilbert only."

Mr. Fling's name was on the card, and Mr. Gilbert said, "Show him up."

Mr. Fling entered, and said something about not expecting to find Mr. Gilbert, but Mrs. Gilbert remarked that her husband knew all.

"And have you then exposed me?" asked Mr. Fling.

"Another visitor!" whispered the servant, bringing a second card. "She want's to see you only."

"Show her up," commanded Mr. Gilbert, and in a moment, Mrs. Fling came sweeping into the room.

There was a great deal of embarrassment, and it required some minutes to bring their minds down to any degree of composure.

Mary broke the ice by asking a question :—

"Mr. Fling, could you assist us in tracing out the parentage of a certain little vagrant, who assisted you in the junk line, some fifteen years ago?"

Mr. Fling changed color, and Mrs. Fling's chin fell an inch.

The conversation soon became general, and before Mr. and Mrs. Fling took their leave, two remarkable facts were made known, in each of their minds. *First:* that Mrs. Fling was the wife of the fugitive junk-shop keeper, who employed Mary to steal when she was a vagrant child. *Second:* that the wife of the fugitive junk-shop keeper was Mary's mother, and consequently, mother-in-law to her husband, Simeon Gilbert, the rich stock jobber.

"And you are really my mother!" exclaimed Mary, giving Mrs. Fling a dutiful embrace.

* * * * * * *

Mr. and Mrs. Fling have both gone to their last account. The money panic, a few years ago, overturned Simeon Gilbert's mind, and he is now in the State Asylum. By the recent death of Mary's grandfather, an English nobleman, she has come into possession of a vast fortune of her own. She is now, perhaps, the wealthiest lady in New York. But, alas! she is far—very far, from being happy.

* * * * *

Mrs. Gilbert is not the only woman now living in New York whose life shows such a remarkable extreme. Though, it generally happens that their transit is down instead of up. Wrong education and fast living, have a tendency to dissipate health and fortune. Indeed, there is no place in the world so likely as a great city, to prove the grave of a woman's ambition. Where one ascends, ten go down; where one poor woman lives to enjoy a happy future in affluence, a dozen idly reared girls drag out a wretched existence of blighted expectations. Last summer, an old woman who sells nuts and apples outside of the City Hall Park, was pointed out to us by a gentleman, who remarked, "She rode in her carriage twenty years ago. I have danced with her myself, at a party in the house of a fashionable friend. She was then wealthy."

"And how is it that she has come to this?" we asked in wonder.

"She was fond of gin, for one thing," replied the gentleman. "And they said she lost a great deal at the gaming table. She was fond of cards, and always played for money, until a sharper fleeced her."

MADAME DE WALL.

MADAME DE WALL:

THE WOMAN IN BLACK.

My passions are all living serpents, and
Twin'd, like the gorgons, round me.—BYRON.

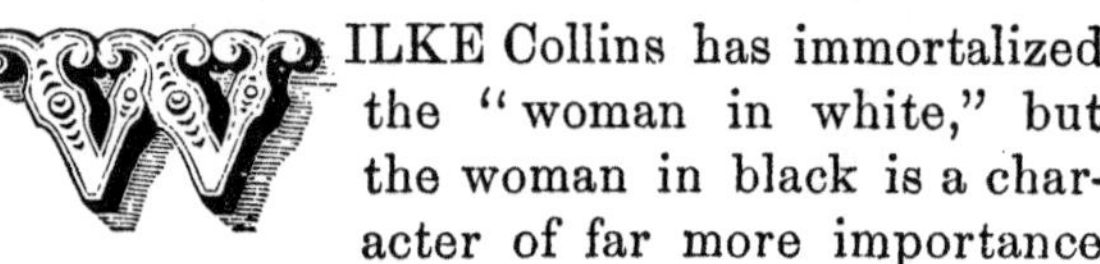

WILKE Collins has immortalized the "woman in white," but the woman in black is a character of far more importance in matters that pertain to the well-being of society. There are numerous classes of women in black, but Madame De Wall is not one of the ordinary kind. In the outset, we will ease the reader's mind by stating that Madame is now a wicked woman. When she was quite young, she naturally fell in love; but, unfortunately for her future good, she did it very unwisely. Instead of being less hasty, and becoming the wife of a worthy man, she thought a little romance would be delightful. In her daily walk to and from school, she passed the window of a picture gallery, where it was her custom to stop and view the pictures therein. Her pretty face attracted the attention of an artist, who contrived to have her sit for a portrait, and it was not long before she and the artist became the best of friends. Hoping to feather his nest by marrying a rich man's daughter, he secretly made her his wife. Had her father known the fact, it is probable that the artist would have lost his life. One year passed, and so did two. The marriage was still kept a secret, but, like thousands of girls have done before, and will ever continue to do, she forgot to destroy one of her clandestine letters, and left it lying in her chamber. A servant carried it to her father, who forthwith inflicted a caning upon the head and back of the artist, for his presuming to write to his daughter. Not dreaming that they were really married, the father set spies to watch the artist and his daughter both, and, in consequence thereof, their intercourse and correspondence were completely cut off. A long interval ensued, during which nothing passed between them, and the artist turned his thoughts upon another pretty face, saying to himself—

"I'll find a mistress elsewhere, and wait for the old man to die. Then I'll take my wife, and some of his brick houses and bright dollars with her."

Two years after that, the father did die. Indeed, we might here remark, and very apropos, that fathers are dying every day, in New York. In a population of one million, there are thousands of fathers, and many of them have daughters, who will soon be left in full possession of the wealth which they have toiled forty or fifty years in accumulating. Daughters of rich old fathers are not long in finding husbands, and in numerous instances, their husbands distinguish themselves by squandering all they can lay their hands on, and then leaving the daughters to murder out the balance of their existence in genteel boarding-houses, or in some other dilemma, the Lord only knows where or how.

Five hundred deaths occur in New York, every week in the year. This is at the rate of seventy a day—or one about every twenty minutes. Every twenty minutes, some wretched mortal is drawing its last breath. Even while we are writing about Madame De Wall, at least one soul has just fled from its tenement of clay in this great city, and gone before the throne of the Eternal, to be adjudged according to the deeds of the body here below. Oh, what misery there is endured at this moment by the inhabitants of this city! How many suffering mortals are now writhing with pains of body and tortures of mind! To pause and reflect upon this terrible truth, would sadden the gayest heart that ever beat! Behold! seventy odd funerals every day! and all here, within a circuit of a few miles. Three new coffins are wanted every hour. As we write, hundreds of men are sawing, planing, pounding and polishing boards of rosewood, mahogany, walnut, cherry or pine, and making them into coffins. Day and night the saw and hammer are continually heard in the workshops of the "undertakers." Strong men work and sweat, and wear themselves out and grow old and die, at their eternal task of making coffins for the dead. Aye, and many a coffin-maker, who has toiled at the trade fifty years, is carried to his grave in a plain box, of simple, unvarnished pine.

Hark! We hear the solemn tones of the great bell in the spire of St. Paul's; and there goes a grand cortege, following the corpse of some rich mortal to its last home in Greenwood.

Then, see that long box, fastened with a rope to the bottom of a dray. The driver looks back at the load with a sort of shrink. He knows what the box contains. Ask him, and he will say, "a dead body!" It is the corpse of a poor man or woman, whose life departed amid poverty. There are no mourners, and it is deposited in the dismal sepulchre appropriated for the bones of the friendless and the poor.

Thousands have died in New York since the corpse of Madame De Wall's father was laid in that beautiful gothic tomb, situated at the south end of Greenwood Cemetery. With his death, came the artist, to claim wife and fortune. But time works wondrous changes.

"No!" said the daughter. "You have acted basely by me. I know of your doings, and will not now be your wife. You have another to love, and I will not abide with you."

"But the law will allow me the right I demand," said the artist. Admitting that love has died out between us forever, we can, at least, appear to be man and wife in the eyes of the world. You are rich—I am poor. You loved me when we stood up before the clergyman; you then vowed to be an obedient and loving wife, until death should separate us. There is now no obstacle to keep us apart."

"All your reasoning will have no avail. I will not be your wife. The clergyman who married us no longer lives, and the proof of a marriage does not exist."

"Yes, but there was a certificate, bearing the

clergyman's signature, and that is a document legal enough to settle the question before a court."

"That certificate you gave to me, and I have reduced it to ashes."

"Not so. I gave you only a copy of the original." The artist took a soiled paper from his wallet, and holding it so that she could read, he continued—"There it is; and you will also perceive the signature of a witness. That witness will testify for *me*."

Forced into it, she yielded with a spirit of hate, which grew more bitter every day. The artist was soon a miserable sot; for, with all the money he could spend, his career was downward rapidly enough. His life was soon finished.

* * * * *

When the artist died, his widow was accused of taking his life, and her accuser was the woman who shared his joy and sorrow while he was waiting for his father-in-law's demise. The woman hated the wife, and it is probable that she really believed the artist had been fatally dealt with. The corpse was disinterred, and the doctors reported, "arsenic, in considerable quantities." The widow had a prospect of serious trouble. The grand jury indicted her, and heavy bonds barely saved her from prison. When the case came on, there were no witnesses against her, and nothing further could be done. Her accuser was "found drowned."

The notoriety of her recent trouble induced her to travel. During her absence, she assumed the name of Madame De Wall, and came back with an ill frown upon her features.

Rumor has had much to do with the name of Madame De Wall. All kinds of stories have been told and related to her discredit, and more than one husband, and perhaps a score of fathers, will look daggers when they see her carriage pass. Her fortune is said to have disappeared soon after her husband; but she has always managed to live, and is never without plenty of money. They say she is ready for anything that will pay, and honesty is not a matter to be considered in her undertakings. In a city like New York, where so much wickedness is constantly carried on, the Woman in Black is looked upon, by *free* thinkers, as a necessary evil. At all events, the city would not be what it is without them.

* * * * * * * *

No sensible reader will imagine, from the revelations in this sketch, that *all* women in black are wicked. We should be sorry to think that, for there are thousands of good, honest souls, eternally clothed in sable attire, who have grief at their hearts, and whose memories are in the deepest mourning. We have profound respect for the black robe, and the long, ebon veil, no matter where we see it, or by whom it is worn. On an old lady, it is always becoming, and significant of the future. But young ladies who prance and giggle, should not put it on, save in actual mourning. Yet, as the white neckcloth of a clergyman has aided many a fraudulent knave to carry out his wicked schemes, under the guise of sanctity, so does the garb of black help a treacherous woman in the accomplishment of her cruel designs. We say cruel, for the reason that we know she is more heartless than a man. Do not start, gentle reader, when we make the declaration that woman, when depraved and lost in crime, has a heart of threefold harder stone than the veriest demon who ever wore the beard of a man. One really wicked woman will sow the seeds of greater crimes than three men can ever do.

MRS. JEWETT.

MRS. JEWETT:

THE BROKEN HEARTED.

"That thou art blamed shall not be thy defect;
For slander's mark was ever yet the fair:
So thou be good, slander doth but approve
Thy worth the greater."

MEN always laugh at the idea of a "broken heart," and we believe that very few women place much faith in possibilities of this kind. And yet, it is said a thousand times a day, in speaking of some wretched one, "She's heart-broken!" The expression is common, but seems only to imply that such a one is overwhelmed with trouble, or full of grief. But, dear reader, there *are* broken hearts in this great city.

* * * * *

Some years ago, we visited the police court one morning with a friend, to see a woman who was to have a hearing upon a charge of poisoning her own child. A notice in the papers, called our attention to the arrest of the woman, and as the circumstances were so remarkable, we desired to look at a mother who could be such a monster, if such a one there really was. Our friend was a lawyer, and enjoyed privileges, whereby he secured a comfortable seat for us, away from the crowd, and while concealed from the eyes of others, we could plainly see all that was going on. After two or three trivial cases were disposed of, the clerk called the name of "Mrs. Jewett." But no answer came.

"Officer, where is your prisoner ?" demanded the magistrate, looking over his spectacles to the far corner of the room.

"Please, your honor, she'll be back directly," cringed an Irishman, approaching the bar. "She was fainten like, and Mahoney and McDuell jest took her back to the matron of the prison. They'll be in with her presently, your honor."

"We can not wait!" growled the magistrate. He twisted in his seat a moment, and then turning to his especial officer, he said :—

"Newmans, go and bring her in. The court is in a hurry. I have business of importance on hand this afternoon, and shall adjourn at eleven o'clock. Cases not disposed of by that time, must lie over until Monday."

The officer bowed low and hurried out. In a moment he returned with Mahoney and McDuell, partly carrying and dragging a woman between them.

"Stand up here!" said the clerk.

The magistrate adjusted his spectacles at the right focus, and prepared to take a thorough scrutiny of the prisoner. She was standing, or rather leaning against the railing, but a veil covered her face, and besides, she held her head down, so that it was impossible to catch the least glimpse of her features. There was a deep silence in the room.

"Madame," said the magistrate, "you will uncover your face,—the court does not wish to deal with one whose features are invisible."

The prisoner sobbed aloud. The crowd held their breath, and gazed sadly on the scene. The prisoner's garments were elegant and costly, and showed that her circumstances were above the general masses.

"Madame," repeated the magistrate, in a harsher tone, "the court wishes you to uncover your face. The court must be obeyed."

Sobs louder than before, followed the magistrate's second order, and he impatiently said to his special officer :—

"Newmans, take that veil off *for* her! Come, we have no time to trifle!"

The magistrate was in a hurry, for he had set his mind upon witnessing the races to come off that afternoon, out on Long Island. He kept fast horses himself, and enjoyed such things very much. The hour he fixed for adjournment was nearly up, and every moment's delay made him uneasy.

The officer touched the prisoner's veil to push it aside, but she clutched it tightly, and it could not be moved without tearing. He hesitated, and glanced towards the magistrate to know what he should do.

"Off with it, Newmans!" roared the magistrate in anger. "No matter, let it tear, if it will!"

The officer bowed, and then his strong grasp quickly made shreds of the veil. Yet, her face was not visible, for the loose drapery of her mantle now served her as an effectual mask.

"Take her away!" stormed the magistrate, rising from his seat. "Lock her up until next Monday, and she'll be more accommodating by that time, I guess. Away with her! The court is adjourned. Newmans, leave her to Mahoney and McDuell, they can manage her: I want you with me."

The prisoner gave a hysterical scream, as

the men took hold of her to drag her back to prison, and we felt very much like scratching the magistrate's face. He put on his hat, and left.

"It's all over for to-day," said our companion. If you still wish to see her, you'll have to come again on Monday."

* * * * * * *

Reader, come with us into a millinery store in Broadway. Do you see that pale-faced lady, behind the counter, yonder? Poor creature! her history is a sorrowful one. You think she has seen much sickness, but, alas! her sunken cheeks and hollow eyes were not made so by disease. Her sufferings have been more of the mind than of the body. We can assure you that her lot has been a bitter one. Until she married Mr. Jewett, her life was one continued summer; but, on the very day of her marriage, trouble began to assail her. The ceremony was hardly performed, when a wicked letter reached her husband, impeaching her character, and laying the foundation of future misery. She knew nothing of the letter, but her husband's manner made her very unhappy. In a week's time, another letter was received, purporting to come from a different writer, with additional slanders. And one day, not a month after their marriage, two men called upon Mr.

Jewett, and stated that his wife had been detected in purloining some valuable laces from the store in which they were employed. He resented the charge, and threatened to pitch them into the street; but, said one of them—

"She has the laces with her. She has not yet returned, and if you will keep your temper, you can prove her guilt by finding them on her person, when she arrives."

Sure enough, when Mrs. Jewett came home, a lot of lace was found under her mantle. She was thunderstruck, and declared that she knew nothing about it. Mr. Jewett went to the store with the two men, and satisfying himself of the theft, he offered to pay for the laces.

"Oh, no," said the storekeeper, "we do not wish you to do any such thing. It's all right, now. But, Mr. Jewett," said the storekeeper, confidentially, "I would suggest that you keep an eye on your wife in future, or she may get into *serious* trouble, where they are not so lenient as I am."

This was only a beginning. Complaints came to Mr. Jewett almost every day, from some new quarter, stating that his wife was doing this or that to disgrace his name. And, upon investigation, the evidence was always conclusively against her, so that longer submission would have been more than human forbearance was capable of. She denied all the charges, and cried herself sick about them so often that her beauty was rapidly fading. When Mr. Jewett made her his wife, she was very pretty, and he really loved her—had he not, he would have abandoned her long before he did. But now, with every proof of her depravity, and a fading of her rosy cheeks, and a dimming of her bright eyes, his attachment was rapidly cooling down.

"Mrs. Jewett," said he, "we must separate. I have loved you too well, but cannot live in this way any longer. My lawyer has instructions to procure a divorce. If you defend it, all your past offences shall, of course, come out to strengthen my cause. If you yield, then you may escape comparatively unexposed. I shall quit New York as soon as the divorce is decreed, and possibly may never return here to live."

Mrs. Jewett had not the courage to resist. Her hopes were all dead, and she made no defence.

When Mr. Jewett was absolved from matrimony, he quit the city, as he proposed, but left their only child with his divorced wife. Soon afterwards, the child died and its mother was accused of taking its life. She was arrested, and a notice of it in the papers drew us to the

Police Court, as we described in the first part of this sketch. We visited the court again on the Monday following, and saw her. Her hearing was quickly over, and she was committed for trial. A jury of men, after listening half a day to the evidence, unanimously agreed upon a verdict of *guilty*, without any appeal to the mercy of the court.

She was remanded for sentence, three days hence. But the second night after her conviction, Judge ——, a worthy magistrate, then presiding in the General Sessions, was suddenly summoned to the bedside of a dying woman. She was nearly gone when he arrived, but still sensible.

"Judge, there is a Bible, on the table," said she. "I wish you to swear me. I have some disclosures to make, and earnestly desire that they should be accepted as the truth."

The Judge administered the oath.

"And now," said she, "you will remember that my testimony was the chief evidence against Mrs. Jewett, in her trial for the murder of her child. My evidence was false! Yes, Judge, false! It was I who poisoned the child, and she is innocent. On my death-bed, believe me, she is not guilty!"

"You are insane," said the Judge. "Calm yourself. It is impossible that you could have had any motive strong enough to make you commit such a horrible twofold crime! It is but the wandering of your disturbed reason."

"No! no! no! I tell you the truth. Oh, Judge! I am dying, and implore you to believe me, and save her from further misery. I have had revenge enough—oh, enough! There is a great load of sin bearing me down, and it will push me into eternal fire. Judge, listen to me. Before Mr. Jewett married her, I loved him, and prayed, and hoped, and tried to be his wife. But I was poor, and he did not understand what a depth of passionate feeling lay in my heart, nor did I then know what a demon it would make of me, if it should not be appreciated and received. I was a domestic in his house, and when he brought his beautiful bride home, a sudden thirst seized me to torture her. I began by writing letters, and, with the assistance of an expert shoplifter, continued my persecutions until Mr. Jewett obtained a divorce. Oh! then I thought I would surely gain his notice; but he was moody, and observed nothing. He quit the city, and did not even bid me good bye. I was now more demoniacal than ever. His slight made me a perfect fiend. I remained in her employ, and nursed the child, and gave it poison; and after it was buried, I caused her to be accused of its death. Oh! Judge, you know what followed. I am now dying, and implore that you will let the innocent mother escape."

Newmans witnessed the disclosures of the woman, and then she died.

* * * * * * *

But the confessions of poor Mrs. Jewett's enemy did not come in time to disabuse her husband's mind. He went to Cuba, and there the fever soon terminated his life.

Mrs. Jewett's history would make an interesting volume, but we must now leave her there behind the counter of that fashionable millinery store, where she is struggling and toiling to gain an honest living. At the age of only twenty-five, there she stands, a broken-hearted woman.

MADAME RAND.

MADAME RAND:

THE FORTUNE-TELLER.

"Lady, throw back thy flaxen hair,
And lay thy brow to the moonlight bare,
Then I'll look on thy stars and look on thee,
And tell thee a tale of thy destiny."

THERE was a time when astrologers were highly esteemed by people of great distinction. Indeed, fortune. tellers have always been more or less consulted, from the earliest ages down to the present time. But, with the introduction of electrical telegraphs and lightning printing presses, superstition should be entirely rooted out, and its place occupied by intelligence and reason. Now, in the nineteenth century, with thousands of railroads, hundreds of steamships, and every conceivable invention of art, there should be more thinking and less dreaming. With free schools all over the land, and three thousand periodicals yearly cast before the people, at prices so cheap that beggars even can afford to read, none should be devoid of learning. Ah, we are repeating the word *should*, while, as an experienced journalist, we know that it is useless to moralize over such things. We have written volumes, explanatory of what *ought* to be, and what ought *not* to be, and, after all our well-meant labor, have discovered that if we wish to gain the attention of our readers, we must entertain and please them, and not take upon ourself the liberty of dictation. We will therefore revert to Madame Rand, who occupies apartments in the second story of a frame tenement, on the corner of two dingy streets, within half a mile of the East river. The first floor is used as a grocery store, where a few stale vegetables, and cheap teas and sugars, etc., are retailed out to a very destitute class of buyers. Liquor is the principal traffic of the grocery. A German artist has painted numerous signs on the outside, announcing what may be had to drink within. But there is no connection between the grocery and Madame Rand. The groceryman's name is painted "Mulligen," in large letters, over the entrance, while, on the doorpost leading up stairs, there is a small tin sign, which reads—"MADAME RAND, *tells of the past, the present, and the future, and may be consulted on all questions of law or love. Young ladies will also be shown the portraits of their future husbands.*"

By ringing the bell, we could easily gain access to Madame's presence. We are half inclined to give the bell a pull, and take a peep up stairs ; but, dear reader, we would not like to be seen coming out again.

However, we must tell you what this old hag once did. A merchant, whom we shall call Krumps, doing business in the lower part of the city, conceived a strong passion for his partner's daughter. She was an only child, and very pretty, and he remembered that he had heard of women who made it a business to entrap young girls, and he applied to Madame Rand.

She first found out the school which the daughter attended, and then she gained admission into it for a young woman named Mollie, about the same age of the daughter. Mollie was to obtain her confidence, and aid the hag.

* * * * * * * *

"It's all working out as you desire," said the hag, in reply to Krumps' urgent inquiries. "Mollie has the girl's mind pretty well prepared, and we shall soon bag the game."

"Mollie ! who's Mollie ?" inquired Krumps.

"Oh, she's one of my most reliable assistants.

She is young, pretty, and seemingly artless, and has such a refined way about her, that I've no difficulty in getting her into companionship with the daughters of the first gentlemen of the city. Why, even now, she is on the most intimate terms with a little beauty, whom I am securing for another patron."

When Krumps left, which he did under cover of an umbrella, on a wet night, the hag opened the door of an adjoining room, and called in Mr. Thornley, who was in a merry humor.

* * * * * * *

"Well, if that wasn't old Krumps!" laughed Thornley. "And, would you believe it, it is *his* daughter you and Mollie are after for me!"

"What!" ejaculated the hag, really amazed.

"Yes! Capital, capital! While old Krumps is employing you to corrupt somebody else's daughter, you are actually deluding his own for me. The best joke I ever knew."

Thornley actually rolled over on the sofa, he was so tickled with his disçovery.

"I did not know that Krumps had any daughters," said the hag, seriously.

"Oh, yes. You see, we chaps don't give our real names; we ain't so green as all that comes to. What name did Krumps give you—eh?"

"Brooks," replied the hag.

"The scoundrel!" exclaimed Thornley. "Why

that's—ahem! Krumps is a villainous fellow, that he is!"

"Oh, go on and finish what you began to say —that your real name is Brooks, and that Krumps has taken it to save his own. I see how it is."

"Well, if you must know, then have it so. My name *is* Brooks."

"And you live in Tenth street?"

"Exactly."

Madame Rand jumped as though she had been struck a violent blow. And well she might—for she discovered that Krumps and Thornley were partners in business, and that she was employed by them to corrupt each other's daughter. Under assumed names, they came to her with exactly similar designs, and the villainy was nearly complete. Her situation was a critical one, and she began to be frightened; but gold was tempting, and she choked her terror down.

"What's up, now?" queried Thornley, noticing her manner.

"Nothing but a confounded pain in my side."

Thornley took his hat and departed.

* * * * *

In Greenwood Cemetery there are two graves, almost side by side. These graves contain the remains of two young girls, who died, it was said, from natural causes. One was the daughter of Krumps—the other was the daughter of Thornley. Madame Rand did all she was paid to perform, and two fathers now live to repent of their evil passions, and mourn over that which all their gold cannot repair. They now know what fools they have been, and when they meet, they dare not look each other in the face.

If parents knew all the terrible mischief made by fortune-tellers, they would never permit their daughters to go near them. A worse class of miscreants do not infest the city.

Three years ago, a beautiful, though weak-minded young lady, was deluded by a fortune-teller into marrying her father's coachman. She was the heiress apparent to great wealth, but the spell of the sorceress was too strong to break, and she refused to listen to parents or anybody but her enchantress and her coachman husband. In rage and despair, the father made a will to her prejudice. He recently died, and it has since transpired that the coachman was really the fortune-teller's own son, the whole affair being a shrewd but unsuccessful plan to gain a fortune. We do not know where the daughter is now.

SOPHIA RENVILLE.

SOPHIA RENVILLE:

THE PERFECT LADY.

> "I think of thee, sweet lady, as of one
> Too pure to mix with others, like some star,
> Shining in pensive beauty all alone,
> Kindred with those around, yet brighter far."

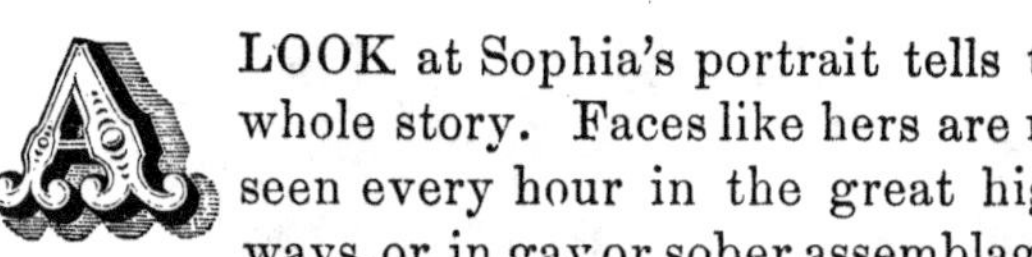

A LOOK at Sophia's portrait tells the whole story. Faces like hers are not seen every hour in the great highways, or in gay or sober assemblages. There is an indescribable grace in Sophia's every movement, which charms the beholder, and commands respect even from those who seldom show deference to any one. Say what you please about the claim *every* woman has to being called a lady, there is a vast difference between the multitude and Sophia Renville. How unlike Miss Jenkins! If "Miss" is not prefixed to *her* name, she is greatly offended, and will plumply tell the person who neglects its use, that, as a lady, she expects to be addressed in proper terms. Such an omission would never annoy Sophia, for, having no desire to be over-estimated, she is entirely free from airs.

Sophia's father is one of the wealthiest merchants in New York, and she rides out daily in the family carriage, with a splendid pair of black horses, and two servants in livery of blue and gold. Her father has erected one of those palaces, which cost a hundred thousand dollars. She is now past twenty, and has seen all that can be seen in the sphere of the fashionable, high-born, and wealthy, and many suitors have tremblingly asked for her hand.

"I don't like her," says Miss Jenkins, who saw her once at the opera. "She is too inanimate for me. I like to see a lady have some life, and she's a perfect stick. She's so very precise."

"You are much mistaken," responds Miss J.'s companion, who, by the way, is a rejected admirer of Sophia's. "Miss Renville is neither inanimate, nor is she a stick ; and I cannot perceive that she is any too precise. She is dignified, and yet, so easy and gentle that no effort is ever visible."

"She's stuck up, though," pouts Miss J.

"Not so," says her companion. "Though

she is considered the belle of the city, and occupies a position far more wealthy than many around her, she is the least assuming lady I ever met with, in all my life."

Sophia's parents were both poor, when they began life together, he twenty-two, and she only nineteen. But that was many years ago. Fortunes are sometimes quickly made, and lost, and made again, in the city of New York. Mr. Renville had barely one hundred dollars to commence on, and now the tax assessor puts him down for several millions. He was the only son of a poor widow, who died in an asylum for the insane, when he was scarcely a year old. He then passed over to the guardianship of a rich old uncle, who endeavored to educate him in the best manner. His uncle lived until he was a fine, promising youth of seventeen, and then suddenly went to his grave, without leaving the nephew a dollar. During infancy, his good nurse, whom he learned to call "Aunty," was, to him, all the mother he ever felt or knew, and he always loved her. But while he was away at school, "Aunty" accompanied some of her friends to a distant part of the world, and he never heard from her again. But the good counsel she instilled into his mind when a child, often restrained him from falling into the temptations surrounding his path through the upward struggle of his life. He married an educated and sensible lady, and no man could love a wife better than he does Mrs. Renville, to this day. Some of his friends say that he adores her. And she merits all the love he gives her. We do not believe there is a happier couple living. We mention the fact as a rare example now-a-days. But Sophia owes much to her parents. Their education fitted them to rear her so as to be worthy of the title of a perfect lady. While they lavished upon her all the accomplishments of the age and the circle in which she was to move and live, they did not forget the more solid branches of learning. She was taught that she must be useful to her fellow mortals, as well as an ornament in the world. To wait upon herself, and to even mend her own clothes, were among the earliest haibts taught her. That she was only mortal, and made of the same flesh and blood that the poorest women are, became fixed in her memory, and with it, the belief that a lady should never treat even the humblest being unkindly. Above all, she was taught to read the Bible, and to fear God. When she was scarcely three years old, she never thought of going to bed without voluntarily getting down on her little knees, and commending her youthful soul to the keeping of her Father in Heaven. Oh, how Mr. and Mrs. Renville have always idolized their sweet child!

"But," said the mother, "we should do our duty, and, despite the pernicious examples which are about us, we must keep close watch on her, and direct her mind into the right channel, that the future may be happy, both for her and for us."

"Yes," replied the father, "we must devote our lives to her, and, while we carefully watch over and instruct her, let us continue to ask assistance and aid from above."

Happy Sophia Renville! She is not like the thousands of her sex who laugh and giggle one moment, and cry and pout the next; nor is she one of the kind who never think of anybody but themselves. When she talks, it is not of herself. There is no egotism or vanity in her. But, had she been reared as the most of girls are, it is very reasonable to suppose that she would now be as short-witted and as ill-behaved as any of them. We do not, for a moment, wish to have it inferred that nature made Sophia Renville such a perfect lady. Oh, no! If she had only what nature gave her, we fear she would have been quite the opposite of what she now is. Left to grow up without proper teaching and good example, the best of us would be far below the standard of a lady. Education is what makes the character, or what developes it, at least. Though, we are not all possessed of the best natural qualities, and it would require a great deal of teaching to make a brilliant lady of a stupid, idiot child. Again, many natures will not toil for advancement, preferring to remain as they are, and live trusting to chance. Parents, and especially mothers, have the future happiness of their children in their hands, and if they are competent to perform their duty well, and will take the trouble and pains to teach them by precept and example, they will not only promote the happiness of the present generation, but benefit their own posterity, and the posterity of others, in ages yet to come.

We could tell many anecdotes, showing wherein Sophia Renville differs so much from the general mass of those who claim to be ladies.

Only the other day, when the pavements were very wet, and the crossings on Broadway so slippery that the surest footed could not stand, an old woman waited on the curbstone to pass over, as soon as there should be any opening between the endless throng of vehicles. She was quite feeble and tottering, and her dress was only a faded calico. Her appearance was poor and wretched. Twice she essayed to cross, but each time she returned, afraid to venture. Once more she stepped down into the slippery mud, and moved as quickly as her strength would permit. She had gone nearly half the distance across, when a brutal Irish "carman," such as infest New York by the thousand, ran his horse against her and threw her down. The brute saw the old woman in time, and yelled out at her, derisively. He saw that she could not run, and he might have turned his horse's head to avoid her; but he kept straight on, and, after striking her, cursed her for being in his way. Just then, a magnificent private equipage was rolling past, and, in less time than we require to write the fact, it came to a sudden halt. A beautiful young lady alighted, and, with her delicate, kid-gloved hands, helped the old woman to stand erect. The lady's costly robe was spread out in the mud, and great spots were daubed over her white lace mantle.

"Get down, Thomas," she called, to the exquisitely attired footman, who sat up in his place by the coachman's side, quite stiff and grand. "Get down here, quickly, and help me assist this poor woman."

Thomas was amazed at the conduct of his lady, and, just then, could not collect his scattered wits. He and John, the coachman, both saw the carman run against the poor woman, but they had no idea that their lady would risk her pretty self, and spoil her elegant apparel, by cutting such a figure in the most public part of Broadway. Thomas looked into John's face, and John looked into Thomas'.

"Thomas! Thomas! Why don't you come down?" cried the lady, seeing that he made no move to obey.

"Yes, ma'am! Coming!" said Thomas, now understanding matters a little better. But he got down very carefully, and stepped on tiptoe, and touched everything with only just the tips of his fingers.

"Why, Thomas! take hold and help her out of the street. Certainly, you need not fear to spoil your livery, when I risk my dress in this way. Come, get her to the curbstone."

A few moments ago, the omnibus drivers and carmen did not care whether they run the old woman down or not, but now that a grand equipage, with its gay-liveried servants and majestic horses stood there, and such a richly dressed lady was in the way, they all turned aside, respectfully, and passed by, extremely curious to know what it all meant.

It required only a moment to regain the curbstone. The coachman drew up to one side, and a multitude began to gather. Some one said: "Go into the store." The hint was a timely one, and the lady acted upon it immediately. Thomas led the old woman in, and she followed. But, had it not been for the fine carriage, and the lady, and her liveried attendants, *that* storekeeper would not have permitted the old woman to enter his doors, at least, in the sorry condition she was just then. He is a selfish man, and has no pleasant corner in his cold heart, save for courting favor with the rich. But, no matter—he did admit her.

"Oh, thank you, dear, sweet angel!" said the old woman, while tears ran down her cheeks. "I am not hurt—only frightened. Thank you! thank you!" And she kissed the lady's gloved hand with no pretended feeling. "I am able to go on, now. But, oh! what a dear, good, kind lady you are, to get out of your fine carriage to help a poor, miserable creature, like me; and then, to spoil all your silks and laces so, in the nasty mud! Oh! I must kiss you again, and again!" And she did kiss her hand, a dozen times.

There were large tears in the lady's eyes, also, but she brushed them away, and slipped three pieces of bright gold into the old woman's hand.

"Accept these, now," whispered the lady,

"and when you need more, come to me. You will find my name and address on this card."

The old woman did not wish to tax her bounty in such a way, and pushed back the gold; but the lady fairly forced the pieces upon her.

"Tell me your name, good lady," said the old woman. "My eyesight is very dim, and cannot make out what is on the card."

"Sophia Renville," replied the lady.

"*Renville!*" exclaimed the old woman, catching her hand. "Not the daughter of *George* Renville, the great merchant—are you?"

"I am his daughter."

"Heaven be praised!" cried the old woman. "I am even now on my way to his store, to see him, and ask him if he will not do a little towards helping along his old nurse, now that she is good for nothing. The daughter of *George* Renville! Oh! I nursed him—'*little Georgey*'—from the hour that he was born until he went away to school. Oh! he'll remember his old 'Aunty,' as he used to call me. He'll remember *me*—aye, that he will! And you are *his* daughter! I knew that you were an angel!" The old woman wept tears of joy."

When Mr. Renville returned to his dwelling that night, he *did* remember the nurse he used to call "Aunty." Sophia had taken the old woman home with her in the carriage, to the great mortification of Thomas and John, who thought it was a rather shabby exploit. Mrs. Renville gave her a warm welcome, but when Mr. Renville saw her, he actually folded his arms around her, and something like tear-drops were in the corners of his eyes, for her presence recalled the days of his childhood, and it seemed as only yesterday that "Aunty" was so good and so kind to him.

Before retiring to bed that night, Mr. Renville knelt beside his old nurse, and prayed, just as she had taught him to when he was a little child. It was a holy picture. The rich man kneeling on the velvet carpet in his mansion, before that poor, old woman, with his devoted wife and their good daughter by his side.

"And now, 'Aunty,'" said Mr. Renville, when he had finished his prayer, "let my house be your home while you live."

* * * * * * *

Judging Mr. Renville by the generality of men in business around him, hardly one in a thousand would ever imagine his true character at home. In Wall street, he is only one of the many, who are but types of each other in dress and manners. Their garments are cut in the latest fashion, and made of costly materials, and their language is always easy and affable. They have a smile and a bow for everybody in the "sphere of money," and stand ready to "negotiate" in any way desired by their customers. Mr. Renville made a fortune by being a "Wall street man," and the outside world have no idea of his true character at home. Knowing what little we do of Wall street, we cannot help ejaculating—"Oh, how unlike other men he is!" Would that there were a few more such as he, and then we should have a different state of morals among the wealthy daughters who make up the "beauty and fashion" of the great city.

* * * * *

Sophia Renville has at last found a heart which seems to beat in unison with her own. *They say* that a wedding will soon take place. If so, we hope her husband will be worthy of such a jewel, and that their wedded life may be a long and a happy one.

MEDORA JACOBS.

MEDORA JACOBS:

THE CONFIDENCE WOMAN.

"A creature of amphibious nature,
On land a beast, a fish in water,
That always preys on grace or sin,
A sheep without, a wolf within."

ITH such a repulsive face, it must require great skill for Medora Jacobs to succeed as a confidence woman. There is not a clever point in all her features, and it is somewhat remarkable to us, that she ever accomplished a single undertaking. Yet, the race she sprang from have ever been noted for their perseverance in anything to avoid actual, legitimate labor, and perhaps this is why she *does* succeed, under the serious disadvantage of her ugliness. We need not say that she is a pure descendant of the ancient Israelites—her countenance shows the fact plainly enough.

It is said that her birth-place was in Mulberry street, and that she manifested some of the striking peculiarities of her character at a very early age. When her old father was put on the witness' stand to testify, in a trial she recently had for false pretences, he stated, among other facts, that she made a collecting tour on her own account, when she was only about nine years old. She persuaded a schoolmate, not so young as herself, to assist her in preparing a written appeal to the humane and charitable, in behalf of a destitute family of small children, whose father had fallen and dislocated his back. Prevailing upon her schoolmate to accompany her, she then applied at the doors of houses in a remote part of the city, and collected several dollars in one afternoon. She repeated the operation as often as she could absent herself from school, which she sometimes did by carrying forged excuses to the teacher. Prudently going into a different street every time she went out, she continued to collect donations until she had accumulated over a hundred dollars. She was cunning enough to keep her money out of sight, and her parents, whose circumstances were comfortable and easy, had no thought that their child was at mischief of any kind. However, Medora was suddenly stopped in her enterprise by a crabbed policeman, who took her to the station house. He had questioned her, a week or so before, and finding that she told him falsehoods, he concluded she must be an impostor, acting under the direction of an older head. The captain of the police tried to make her tell where she lived, but she refused to answer any questions. He then opened a cell door, and told her she must be locked up in there, unless she answered. Other children would have screamed, and begged off, and freely disclosed anything asked them, but Medora only bit her lips and hung down her head.

"She's a hard little case," said the captain, to one of his men, "and I don't believe it possible to get anything out of her."

"Set her at liberty again," whispered the man. "The chances are that she will go straight home. It is an easy matter to follow her."

"Good!" coincided the captain. Then approaching Medora, he said—"Now, my girl, if you'll promise me to go home, and never be caught out in the same way another time, I'll let you off. What do you say to that—eh?"

Medora only gave a single affirmative nod. She did not move her tongue. The door opened, and she darted off, followed by one of the men, who endeavored to keep his eyes on her, without being seen. The trick was successful, and Medora was traced home. Her father had much difficulty in settling the matter.

At the age of fourteen, Medora quit her father's roof entirely, and resorting to different guises, she imposed upon all classes of people. Among the first of her victims was a boarding-house keeper. She represented herself to be the daughter of some great man of wealth, and thus obtained not only the best rooms in the house, but actually borrowed various sums of money. When the boarding-house keeper found out the swindle, there was a terrible rumpus; but Medora coolly packed her trunks, and deliberately had them removed, before the eyes of her victim.

"Oh, you cheat!" stormed the aggrieved.

Medora smiled, and replied thus:—

"Well, Madame, you see there is no law permitting you to keep my trunks, and as I may want them myself, I'll just take them with me. Good day, Madame; I shall be delighted to call again."

It would fill a thousand pages like these, to relate the impositions of Medora, and therefore we can select only a few of them. A very common trick of hers was to apply at a new hotel, where she had never been known, or to a boarding-house, and engage the best rooms for herself and husband, and sometimes a few children, and a servant or two. She proposes to come immediately, but, as her family are out of the city, they will not arrive for a week or ten days. She dresses magnificently, and has a great number of diamonds. A whole cart-load of trunks come with her, and no one would dare presume that she was not a woman of wealth and high connections. The best the house can afford is placed before her, and she enjoys herself very much. A week or ten days pass, and no husband arrives, nor do any other members of her family, and she puts on a serious face to appear disappointed. Possibly she may shed a few tears, when two or three more days have passed, without bringing her dear " George," or her dear "Nathan." And she so wants to see her youngest boy, "Botty." " Oh, what *has* happened!" she grieves, loud enough for the ears of *some* one, if it's only the chambermaid. She inquires repeatedly and urgently for a letter. " None! no letter, either?" she exclaims, incredulously. " Oh, there must be something wrong—I'm sure there is " I'll go to the post-office, and see what is there."

" 'Tis kind of funny," thinks the person she is duping. " She said *they* would be here in a week, and it's now nearly a month. I don't know about it; and I begin to want my pay; her little bill is considerably over a hundred dollars, now."

But Medora gets a letter, at last, and then she jumps and dances for joy.

"It's all right! nothing is wrong; only detained longer than he expected to be. Now I shall see dear Nathan and little Botty!

She kisses the letter, and seems so happy.

Two weeks more pass, and no "dear Nathan" nor "little Botty" arrives. The truth begins to dawn, and a sharp voice demands the payment of a large bill for rooms and board.

"Oh, I can't pay it till Nathan comes," replies Medora, with mingled regret and indignation. "I never pay such bills; *he* always attends to them himself."

Again Medora moves, to try her luck elsewhere. Meanwhile, she is practicing all manner of tricks upon storekeepers and shopmen, to get possession of goods without paying money for them. She gets sixty dollar mantles, five hundred dollar furs, seventy dollar robes, and hundred dollar 'kerchiefs, to say nothing about the endless variety of et ceteras, in the way of under-clothing, and shoes, and gloves, all for nothing but skillful falsehoods and shrewd calculations. It is very seldom that she is actually circumvented; should she be, it is an easy matter to pay a small bill now and then, and settle any case that threatens to be dangerous and troublesome. Nine-tenths of what she gets possession of, goes almost directly to an acquaintance of hers, who keeps a pawn-shop in the Bowery ; and in this way, she continually increases her stock of money. And it is a rule of hers, never to let an acquaintance slip unfleeced. She borrows of everybody she can. At first, she will ask for only a small sum, and return it promptly ; then she will borrow again and again, gradually increasing the amount, and returning it so faithfully that she can readily get a larger sum. When she has reached what she considers the extreme amount, she suddenly neglects to return it as before, and another victim is added to the list already so long.

The reader may well ask, how a woman with a face like Medora Jacobs' can be so successful as a trickster. We have asked ourself the same question, and the only way we can account for it is, that she was never known to *look cross or to speak unpleasantly to any one.* She is peculiarly insensible to many little influences which would irritate, annoy, and really distract other women, and can, therefore, keep tranquil under the most exciting circumstances.

There is much power in a smile. We have

seen frightfully ugly women gain friends upon all sides, by smiling sweetly and speaking gently, when, if they had not spoken or smiled at all, they would have been set down as very disagreeable persons. Beauty is a great assistance for a woman in her journey through life, whether she has her own living to provide for or not; but unless it is accompanied with winning smiles, gentleness of speech and placid demeanor, it cannot avail her much in the hour of difficulty. A beautiful woman is also more liable to be suspected of fraud than she would be if downright ugly. There seems to be a general suspicion in the minds of a great majority of New Yorkers, that every pretty woman they see who is not possessed of an independent income or supported by some relative, must certainly be a sharper—more particularly if she happens to be a stranger.

Spiteful remarks uttered against pretty women are so common, that if we were influenced by what we hear, it would be impossible to believe that honesty and beauty ever existed together beyond the sight of parents or relatives. The reader may think us a little too severe, but we know that many and many a good, honest woman, unfortunately possessed of a pretty face and comely form, and having herself to maintain, has been seriously disgraced by the malicious tongues of spiteful old maids and girls, and revengeful mothers, and more fatally so by the heartless winks and hints of young men and gray-haired sinners, who wish to appear important among their companions. Only the other day, a man whose wife was at one time in really very bad repute, remarked, in the presence of a table-full of guests at a hotel, that a certain married lady, who formerly boarded there with her husband, was "a hard case."

"A hard case!" responded a gentleman who heard the remark. "Why do you say that?"

"Well, her husband doesn't live with her, and there must be some cause for it."

"Do you *know* anything against her?"

"Oh, no;—but they say she is not what she ought to be."

"*Who* say so?"

"Friends of mine."

"Did they say they *know* anything against her?"

"No; they only said they had *heard* so."

The man appeared to think that he was doing a clever thing, and smiled meaningly to those who sat near; but the gentleman he conversed with thought differently, and, by way of a lesson, went on to lecture him thus:

"It is very easy, sir, to cast reflections

against an innocent woman: and from a single careless or heartless remark, bye and bye thousands may be repeating what you have just said, that '*she is not exactly what she ought to be,*' or, that '*she is a hard case,*' until, eventually, the whole community actually believe the slander, while she, good and pure, with no thought that such terrible mischief is at work blasting her reputation, innocently wonders why men stare at her so rudely, and why women look at her askance. What if I, or any man, should hear another say that *your* wife is 'not what she ought to be,' or that 'she is a hard case,' and should go on repeating it in the hearing of others? Suppose, sir, that even *now*, the people around you are remarking the same things against your wife, behind your back—what would you think of *that?*"

The subject was suddenly dropped, for the man left his dinner unfinished, and went out to take a little air. And as he withdrew, at least twenty grinning countenances looked after him.

Oh! slander is a cruel injury! And it seems to us that one half of the people of New York want no better amusement.

But such women as Medora Jacobs seldom get slandered or abused without the most substantial causes. In the first place, she is too ugly to attract the notice of *smart* young men, and if she did, none of them would care to boast of knowing anything about her, either good or bad. In the second place, her beauty never excites the enmity of her own sex, and as she is forever smiling on them, and talking so blandly, and doing all manner of little kindnesses to win their confidence, she runs no risk in that quarter. The only people who say bitter things against Medora Jacobs, are those whom she has duped. Among her associates are no enemies, for she retains the friendship of all as long as she can, and then parts with their society forever, carrying with her the most valuable tokens of their former regard, in the shape of borrowed clothes or money.

But all Confidence Women are not precisely after the pattern of Medora Jacobs. There are a great many very pretty young widows, and fascinating ladies, who scorn honest employments, and subsist entirely upon what they can gain by their *wits*. Yet, their experience is just the reverse of Medora's, for, being attractive to the opposite sex, and obnoxious to their own, they are sure to get into frequent dilemmas. Indeed, they are so *sought* after by the one, and *persecuted* by the other, that they have hardly a fair chance to test their ingenuity as Medora does. But, as a general rule, we believe that *pretty* Confidence Women, on the average, do not take in their victims as badly as they get taken in themselves.

It is quite easy for a skillful physiologist, or student of city life, to distinguish a Confidence Woman, and it is only over-credulous or thoughtless people who get taken in by them.

Medora thus explains one of her best plans :

"Only just get 'em to think they'll make something from you," says she. "Just get 'em to calculating the profit you'll be to 'em, and, ten chances to one, they'll let you have it all your own way. Money'll blind the best of 'em," says Medora. "So, while they are feeling for your portemonnaie, just you peep into all their pockets."

* * * * * * *

Medora Jacobs is now doing penance out in the country. She did not go there of her own accord. Some of her victims resolved to "join issue," and bring her to justice. In a body, they were too much for her, and she is now safely locked up in Sing Sing prison.

MISS JOHANNAS.

MISS JOHANNAS:

THE BOGUS LADY.

" 'Tis not in folly not to scorn a fool,
And scarce in human wisdom to do more."

IT often happens that cars and stages are full of passengers; but when Miss Johannas enters, it is certainly expected on her part, that somebody shall instantly rise and offer her a seat. Occasionally, there is nobody in the humor of doing so, and then she will walk through the car, or stand up in the stage, and look like a thunder cloud. If her frown is not sufficient to frighten a man out of his seat, she says to Miss Dumps, her companion :—

" They're not gentlemen, that's quite plain. You wouldn't 'spect anything better of sich as *them*."

She speaks mutteringly, but loud enough for

the hearing of others, and glances at the nearest gentleman, as though she would be highly delighted to kick his shins.

Possibly, an old gentleman, with a ruddy complexion, and gold headed cane, motions her to sit upon his knee, and she does not wait for a second invitation, but plumps herself all over his lap, and thrusts her furs or her mantle into his face, and almost smothers him. She's none of your mincing paragons of modesty, to content herself just on the tip of the gentleman's knee, and all the time feeling as though she ought to apologize for sitting there at all, not she. Miss Johannas looks upon herself as a *lady;* and she wishes it to be distinctly understood by everybody she meets, that she is rather above the average. But, unfortunately, Miss Johannas's ideas of what constitutes a lady are frightfully erroneous. Her mother before her, had just such notions, with the exception that she is very much ahead of her mother. She has been taught, that ladies are something to be sought after and admired by the entire whiskered gender.—That no man should so far forget the duties of a gentleman, as to think of his own person, or the comfort thereof, when a lady needs his assistance, or deserves his courtesy. A man is only a man, but ladies are quite different beings. They are angels, to be petted, caressed, and adored by gallant beaux, and afterwards elegantly maintained by indulgent and munificent husbands.

Miss Johannas is now and then shocked at the conduct of other females, and, to our positive knowledge, she has expressed herself in this wise, more than once :—

" Oh, dear ! how *some* ladies *can* behave so, I don't understand. *My* sensibilities is too delicate, and my feelings is too refined. to act as they do."

And while Miss Johannas is trying to find a defect in the conduct of another, she puts all modesty to blush, by her quick and alarming familiarity with a gentleman, introduced to her only a moment ago. The words of introduction are hardly spoken, before she rushes at the stranger, exclaiming—

" Glad to make your acquaintance, sir. Happy to have that pleasure. How do you *do* ? Dear, me ! it's sich a warm day, and has been since last night. I always suffer with the heat so !—why just feel of my hand !—see how very moist it is !—oh, I sweat so terribly !"

She stares directly into his eyes, and feels sure that she is fascinating him. He, completely nonplused, is only able to mumble out a feeble response, ere she starts off again. In less than half an hour, she will have him by the arm, and when she fancies she has said something very clever, she will clap him playfully on the knee, or push him, or dig her straightened-out fingers into his shoulder, or his short ribs. She manifests such violent paroxysms of mental hydrophobia, that you begin to wonder whether she really intends to eat him, and is only waiting for him to melt, and then take him in a liquid state, or whether she is watching for a favorable opportunity to swallow him whole. Just now, it matters very little to her, whether he is rich or poor, low-born or genteel. She is delirious with conquest, and feels insanely happy in the delusion of the moment. He, poor fellow, can not get a chance to speak. If she asks him a question, she also rattles out a reply before he can say a word. Her tongue goes until she is out of breath, and then she takes a long respiration, and continues to fly on. Her whole talk is about herself.

Our readers may think this picture exaggerated, but if they could only see her as we have seen her, they would say that we are not half up to the mark. When there are several persons in the room, ladies and gentlemen together, she is sure to answer any and every question, that may be asked. No matter if Mr. Hooper should say something to Miss

Brent, a reply will come from Miss Johannas. The truth is simply this: Miss Johannas forgets that there is another person besides her own dear self, in the whole world. Whatever is to be had, she expects to get: if any body is to be complimented, it should be her. Miss Johannas is every thing and every body, and as perfect as an angel. So her mother says, at any rate; and it is reasonable to suppose that mothers should know more than any body else, about their *own* daughters.

Miss Johannas is ever on the look out for presents, and frequently gets a ring, a fan, a breastpin, a pair of gloves, or other trifle from some *new* beau; but those who have enjoyed her acquaintance for any length of time, do not compliment in that way. Miss Johannas says that when she gives up single life, she expects to marry "somebody,"—no common man will do for her. He must be tall, handsome, and of the most polished manners, and be able to support her *and* her mother, in the style they should be. Miss J. is only a poor girl, the daughter of a widow, who has hard work to make her income supply all her wants, and if she *can* get a handsome, polished man, able to keep her *and* her mother, as she talks about, we are quite willing; but, to give our candid opinion, we should say that no polished man of sound mind, will ever marry her; and as it is not a stipulation in the marriage contract, to maintain mother-in-laws, we may also predict that she will be disappointed there too. To come down to the truth, Miss Johannas is neither fit to be the wife of a gentleman of fortune, nor a help mate for a poor man. She is ambitious enough, in all conscience sake, but intrinsically, she is worth very little now, and will decrease in value the longer she lives. If she ever does marry—(and by the way she *will*, some day, very suddenly, on purpose to spite her previous lovers, if for no other reason)—she will make a miserable life of it for the man whose admiration for her large eyes, and red lips, made him forget what merits are requisite in a wife.

We saw Miss Johannas riding in a Broadway stage, the other day. It is universally known, that six persons may sit on either side of an omnibus, but she occupied the space usually allotted for four, thereby compelling three men, and one woman with an infant in her arms, to stand. And the most remarkable part of her impudence, was the fact that she tried to do a little eye-coquetting with one of the gentlemen her ill manners compelled to stand in such a position that he was bumping his head every now and then.

It is difficult to imagine what the destiny of Miss Johannas will be, for with a face so fresh and pretty, and having such a wonderful stock of assurance, there is no telling what good fortune, or bad luck may lie in her path. We know many instances of preferment, wherein *real* ladies have been thrust aside, and *bogus* ones accepted.

* * * * * * *

A bogus lady may have a tolerably pleasant time of it, while her face retains its freshness and natural beauty ; and, indeed, she may keep up the semblance of youth, for some years after the real bloom of her cheeks has faded. It costs only a trifle to buy a box of lily white, and a bottle of vinegar rouge, and she learns very aptly how to " put them on." Until her eyes sink too far into their sockets, these simple colors can do much towards her external preservation. Of course she will be obliged to resort to such remedies, when her cheeks grow sallow, for having nothing but *looks* to depend upon, she will soon be pushed aside, and get no notice. She was never taught that any thing more than looks were required by a *lady*. The mere fact that she was of the feminine gender, and rather prepossessing, was quite enough to build upon. *Education* was not thought of by her mother, and she had very little desire for knowledge, beyond what pertained to dress and parties. She was born a lady, and had no need of any finishing touch from art. Who could help admiring her, and what nice young man would not have gone into "conniptions," at the prospect of getting *her* for his wife? But she fades, and sallows, and wrinkles, and may find a husband at the eleventh hour, when she can no longer choose. Ah, a very little while will make her sour and crusty. Her husband must take to lager beer and billiards, or become a politician, if he expects to get any more pleasure in *this* life. With nothing but a *face*, the bogus lady may begin high spirited, and entertain colossal expectations, and after a brief struggle, find herself moping in misery and disappointment, with a husband who does not believe in angels, and three cross children to nurse. Ah, we'll not trace her up any farther, lest we find an unpleasant picture.

JULIA MORRIS.

JULIA MORRIS:

THE ADVENTURESS.

"To be honest as this world goes,
Is to be one man pick'd out of ten thousand."

But at sixteen the conscience rarely gnaws
So much, as when we call our old debts in
At sixty, and draw the account of evil,
And find a deuced balance with the devil.—BYRON.

WE will let Julia tell her own story :—

"I was born," she says, "in the country, but do not know the exact day or year. Though I do know that I never fancied being a DEPENDENT in my uncle's house, where I was compelled to mend my own dresses, and darn my own stockings, and then make myself generally useful, by assisting "aunt" in the daily routine of putting the parlor and the chamber to rights, and in the performance of a miscellaneous variety of domestic sewing. When father and mother were alive, I never thought of mending my own clothes; my mother always did it for me: sometimes grandmother would. I don't believe in being a *dependent*, any how. Uncle Josiah was a good, clever man, and always treated me kindly, in *his way;* but then even kindness from some folks, is about as unsatisfactory as the down-right coldness of strangers. As to aunt Sarah, she had no more sympathy in her than a loaf of rye bread. She *may* have shown a little feeling when she *wanted* to, but one thing certain, *I* never found any in her. They said she was very fond of her daughter Mary, before she died, and I guess all her affection was buried at the funeral. Why, I never heard a laugh, nor saw a smile once a month, in uncle Josiah's house. It was nothing but gloom, just in the Quaker style. Precisely 'thee' in every thing. Even the cats, the dog, and the pigs, were expected to use 'plain speech' when they made a noise. Uncle Josiah had four mules among his other stock, and I never heard either of them neigh, but what aunt Sarah would say they were a very profane sort of animal, any how. Oh, I have seen so many cold faces, and heard so many cold salutations, of 'how does thee do?' and listened to so many chilling adieus, spoken in whining 'farewells,' that I almost shudder at the recollection of them. About me, were none but the same sober voices, and melancholy faces, with no warm-hearted companion to converse with, and I grew sad and desolate within. I naturally took to crying, but soon tired of that ; and one morning, while I sat unpicking a tangled skein of sewing silk, a fatal thought entered my mind. There is a bright, happy world, beyond the atmosphere of this Quaker dwelling, and what if I should leave uncle and aunt, and go and try my fortune in the same way that others do? I thought this over all day, and when I lay down that night, my heart was much more buoyant than it had been for a long time. To-morrow, I shall begin preparing for departure. I then had no idea of earning my living,—indeed, did not know that I could do it, if I should try. My plans were soon perfected, and I left the gloomy abode, without saying a word to a single being. No one saw me leave!—no one, except I mention Rover, a good old dog, who had enough affection in him to fill the entire hearts of a hundred women such as aunt Sarah. Poor Rover had been my warmest friend, and found in me a full return of feeling, for he and I were seldom far apart, and nothing ever pleased him better than to lie upon the floor, when I helped aunt Sarah sew, and have me put my feet on top of him. If I moved my feet, he would wake out of his nap, and look up to see what had happened. At night, he always slept either in my bed room, or by the door in the hall. Uncle and aunt both said that it was any thing but lady-like, to have a Newfoundland dog tagging after me wherever I went, but their notions in that particular did not break my heart. Sometimes aunt took it into her head, that the dog should not be lying round the house so much, and then she would say, 'Go out doors, Rover—go long out.' But if he saw 'no' in my face, he never budged an inch; and if aunt attempted to drive him, a fierce growl and a sight of his terrible tushes, would at once put an end to her undertaking. Well, as I was saying, no one but Rover saw me quit the house; and I was not aware that he knew it, until after I had gone nearly two miles on my road to the village where I expected to meet the stage. I then discovered that he was following me. He touched the cold tip end of his nose against my hand, and fairly frightened me. I turned with a frown, and began to scold him; but the poor fellow crept along with his body almost on the ground, and looked so sorry and miserable, that I could not drive him back. But what was I to do?

To take him with me was impossible. I had only a few dollars, and perhaps barely enough to carry me to the city. The trouble and expense of a great animal like Rover, I naturally reasoned, would be more than I could manage.

"Rover's presence started me to thinking, and I sat down at the root of a large oak tree and covered my face to weep. I thought over all my past life, and recalled my days of infancy, (which I can still remember—oh, how vividly!) and my dear mother, who died before my eyes in a fit, when I was in my fifth year, and father, who soon joined my mother in the other world. I thought over everything that had been connected with my life. I was now only seventeen, and what my destiny might be, also troubled me much. I had a good heart,—at least I thought I had,—and I desired to merit the respect of every body. Indeed, I was in a confused state of thought, with honest feelings uppermost, but still bent on venturing out into the uncertainties of what I then fancied to be a bright and cheerful world. I had read only a few books, and but three of them were novels. The periodicals taken by uncle Josiah, were of a kind poorly calculated to inform an inexperienced mind of anything except the doctrines and discipline of Quakerism. One, I think, was called 'The

Friend,' another 'The Banner of Truth,' and a third, 'The Friend's Miscellany.' They were dry reading, and I seldom looked in them.—A neighbor, a man of the world, as uncle used to say, took a city newspaper, which contained stories and other interesting matter, and I made a visit to that neighbor's house every week, on purpose to get a chance to read it. Another neighbor, a man of the world too, was a subscriber to a popular magazine, and I had some excuse to go there, as often as the magazine came. Neither uncle nor aunt had any idea that I was reading the entire contents of those worldly publications, or they would have lessened the number of my visits, very quickly. But I must confess that I gleaned more useful knowledge from them, than I ever did in any other way, before I ventured abroad. I may have imbibed some of the evil contained in them; but as their columns were always stored with a greater preponderance of good, I am quite thankful for what I gained. To those periodicals I then owed all my knowledge of the outer world, and hoping for the best, with no dreams of evil, I had now begun my adventures. How I cried there alone, at the root of the old oak tree. My tears ran down, and poor Rover, who sat upon his hunches as near me as possible, and looking at me pitifully, at last ventured to lick a truant drop from my hand. That little act of Rover's roused me. I hugged his great, shaggy head, and said all the affectionate words I could think of. Then, arranging my attire, I put on the crossest expression I knew how to, and bade him 'go home.' I stamped my foot at him, and started. I looked back now and then, and, as far as I could see him, he still stood in the same position I left him, and gazing mournfully after me. Oh, how my heart smote me for leaving him behind! But what could I do? It was the *first* cruel act forced upon me by the circumstances of my life. Presently I crossed a hill, and the top of it hid Rover from my sight. I then mustered all my resolution, and hastened towards the village. But upon looking back once more, when I had gone full half a mile, what should I see standing in the road on the top of the hill but Rover, still gazing after me!

* * * * * * *

"Ah, seven years have passed since I last saw Rover standing on the top of that hill gazing after me. Seven years are a long time. Little did I then know where I should now be. I need not tell you what I have felt or seen during these seven years. My experience, I now have good reason to know, is just what any other girl would have met with under the same circumstances. If I have any wisdom now, I can assure you that I bought it all, and for some of it I paid a very great price. Many persons will ask why I do not disclose all my experience in those seven years, but I cannot gratify them. Very few people, and especially young adventuresses such as I am, would like to lay bare all the mysteries of their career. Although there is nothing very bad in my experience, there are many things I cannot mention. Look at my portrait, and then reflect upon what I have already told you, remembering the fact that I *am*, at this moment, living by my wits, and perhaps your own conclusions will be near enough to the truth. I have never deliberately wronged any one, nor was I ever guilty of fraud or deception. If people have been deceived in me, the fault was all their own. If I have always accepted and retained what has been given me, it is no more than the purest and the best are doing every hour. If the donor's object and purpose is bad when he gives, that does not defile the gift. We have no right to question the motives of any one. But if the donor loses his gift, and does not gain the object for which he gave, it only proves that he made a bad calculation. And how many men make bad calculations when they think a diamond ring can secure the voluntary acquiescence of whoever they choose to flatter with their munificent bounty! I often think it is very funny why so many men stand ready to pay all my bills, and to present me with the most costly apparel, and even to loan me money, if I but hint that I need assistance, when their wives are frequently without a nice bonnet to attend church in, or their own daughters, quite as interesting as I am, I'm sure, have not got an unsoiled silk to wear. They owe me nothing, for I never saw them before. They are not all very rich, and none of them say what return I am to make for their favors. It is funny—I will leave you to decide if it is not very funny, why so many men treat me in the most extravagant style, entirely reckless of cost, while those who have claims upon them, and who really love them, at home, are actually sighing for their attention, and would be a thousand times happier to get even a single smile from them, than I should be if they were to sacrifice all their property, and their lives beside, for me. Oh, I do not claim to be an angel, nor would I be considered a saint. Indeed, I doubt if I have even the respect of my own sex, or the real admiration of the opposite gender; for, on my knees, I might call God to witness my innocence, and yet none would believe me. I have trifled with this one, and tampered with that one, until all begin to despise me ; and, though there is no one who *can* point his or her finger at me and say *guilty*, yet they all believe that if they cannot, there are enough others who could, if they would. Ah! when a woman thinks she is the gainer by receiving costly gifts from men without any return, she is really losing a hundred fold more than she gets. They lose gold—she loses reputation. They gain wisdom—she gains only what they lose.

"In the day of settlement, when all our accounts are cast up, then I know I shall hide my head and weep. Ah! if I could but banish that dreadful thought of judgment *eternal*, when I am dead,

'How sweetly could I lay my head
Within the cold grave's silent breast,
Where sorrow's tears no more are shed,
No more the ills of life molest.'"

CONCLUSION:

A CONFIDENTIAL SERMON.

Ah, me! woman contains within herself
The seeds and sources of her own corruption;
The cankering rust corrodes the brightest steel;
The moth frets out our garments, and the worm
Eats its slow way into the solid oak;
But Idleness of all evil is surely worst,
The same to-day, to-morrow, and *forever*—
Saps and consumes the heart in which it *works*.

"ONCE upon a time," as ancient "story tellers" used to write, there was a certain clergyman, who spent his days in trying to promote the well-being of those who would listen to the gospel. As a Christian, he knew all that was needful, but the deceits and trickeries of the great world were quite beyond his learning. He was conscientious and religious, and sympathized with his "flock," and encouraged them in doing right.

Now, in the same village where the clergyman lived and taught the gospel, there likewise dwelt a comely widow, who had an only child, and he often found himself thinking of her, with an irresistible inclination to gaze upon her fair face, when "they met by chance, in the usual way." Indeed, he succeeded in winning her over to become a member of his church. He imagined that would satisfy him, but he was mistaken; and so he went on thinking.

The fair widow's only child fell sick, and the physician said to her:—

"I cannot save its life. Alas, it must die!"

Then the clergyman repaired to the widow's house to sympathize and to pray.

"'Tis mine, sweet one!" the mother said,
As her child lay at rest;
She smiled as she gazed on its cherub form
And fondly her babe caressed.

"Not so! 'tis mine!" with chilling voice
Howled the tyrant, Death, so grim;
As he snatch'd the child from its mother's arms,
Thinking naught could baffle *him.*

"What, ho, there—demon!" an angel spoke,
Laying the grim monster low;
"My Master hath need of *this* spotless lamb,
Ere sin shall defile its breast.
It must dwell in that 'better land' on high,
Where alone is peace and rest."

The angel vanished, and the widow's child was dead.

And the clergyman took the widow's hand in his, and said :—

"Weep not, thou afflicted one,
Check the gushing of thy sad tears;
Look up in simple faith to Heaven,
And pray for strength to bear thy grief
In calm resignation.
"Let *me*
With gentle touch efface those tears
That quiver on thine eyelashes,
And let thine eyes gaze into mine—
Mine, which while yet I speak to thee
Are moist from very sympathy.
Pray weep not, unhappy one—
Take *me* close home to thy heart,
And I'll *share* thy grief with thee—
Let us be *one* in sorrow."

The widow's child was carried away to its grave, and she, in proper time, became the clergyman's wife.

Worldly as it may seem, the widow not only became the clergyman's wife, but she also bore him a daughter. It was a cunning little elf, and quickly got into mischief as it learned to toddle about.

"Oh, now I am doubly blest, and very, *very* happy!" murmured the clergyman to his wife.

"'Tis well," she replied. "*This* darling shall comfort me for the cherub that died."

How quick the transit from the cradle to the grave and how soon the child grew to riper years. The cunning little elf changed into a pretty Miss, in her teens.

"'Twas but yesterday," said the father, "that our daughter wore baby clothes, and now she is a full-blown rose. Ah, methinks the heart of man will beat quickly when she comes near."

"Yes," replied the mother, "the years have speedily flown, and our precious darling has womanly grown."

But there was one great defect in their daughter's education. Although himself so good a man, and his wife quite as proper as he, yet in their love they neglected to encourage in her a spirit of Industry—the best of principles—and so, like too many others, in idleness she matured. Her parents were poor; for the gospel was their only revenue, and the people where they lived paid very little for preaching. Idleness begot Vanity, and *then* falsehood came in to cover up imaginary defects. She would not cultivate her mind, but grew up a beauty to the eye, and an icicle to the heart. She did not even read the stories in literary periodicals, which, of the better class, if *used*, and not *abused*, tend to serve an excellent purpose, for they will educate the *heart*, encourage its loftiest and purest feelings, while teaching the heroism of bearing rightly the trials of every-day life. (We ignore the class of novels which excite improper or unhappy feelings, and from such books the honest-hearted reader should ever shrink.) The clergyman's daughter seemed to care only for dress, and to attract attention. IDLENESS was her bane, and in the common phraseology of female vanity, she uttered falsehoods in every sentence. Being poor, she constantly did and said things for outward appearance, to conceal the plain truth, just as thousands of young ladies, aye, and old ones too, are doing at this very moment all over Christendom—pretending to be what they are *not*. Who ever heard a would-be lady *admit* that she was poor, or obliged to depend upon herself for support? Why, out of every hundred poor *girls*, who are daily applying for some employment more genteel than common work, at least ninety-nine, when they enter, will twist and try to affect an apology for making the application.

"I thought I'd try something of the kind—just for amusement, only. I am not *obliged* to; I live with my relations."

You'll surely look at them in doubt. Their garments are seedy, and there is nothing in their features, their manner, or their speech, to show that they are either educated or refined more than the general masses, and you naturally ask—

"Who do you reside with?"

"My uncle."

"Ah! Your uncle is an old bachelor—wealthy and retired?"

"Oh, no; he has a family; a wife, three boys, a little girl and a baby. He is in business down town."

"Indeed! A merchant, or a banker?"

"Neither. He has a situation in a hardware store".

You mentally ejaculate—"A salary of twelve dollars a week!" (You know he can't get more.) And this young *lady* to maintain, in addition to his own numerous family, while *she* says she's not *obliged* to do anything! How *can* she stand there and talk so? *Why* should she deny the truth? We will tell you. It is her Vanity. IDLENESS has taught her to deceive. Why, there are thousands of "would be ladies" in this great city who really *earn* their living in some way, who would risk actual starvation sooner than the *world* should *know* that they are *obliged* to *work*. They entertain a horrible fear of being looked upon as poor, or industrious, or useful. They would rather lodge in an attic, and dine on a crust, and se-

cretly toil twenty hours per diem, and have fashionable garments when they are seen in public, than to be full fed and plainly *what they are*, in an honest, straight forward way. It is astonishing how many females suffer hunger and cold from this one cause, when, if they would but cast off their detestable Vanity, they might easily earn a good, comfortable living, and have the respect of all honest people. Vanity is far from *true* pride.

But this source of evil is not confined to any one class—it is universal. We perceive a similar spirit manifested whichever way we look. And why? Simply because girls, whether rich or poor, mature with the belief that they are ladies, *as a matter of course*, and that as such, they should be appreciated by their own sex and courted by the other. And they believe that it is beneath the dignity of a lady to engage in any useful occupation as a *necessity*. In their estimation, it is more genteel to *stealthily* operate on a sewing machine day and night in a garret, out of sight or hearing of their neighbors and the world, for four dollars a week, than it would be to accept a genteel situation yielding three or four times as much compensation, and have *everybody to know it!* However, Vanity brings its own reward, and they will eventually learn that very little happiness can be gained by their mistaken notions.

If the reader will pardon us for this digression, we will now return to the clergyman's daughter. Though, by way of apology, permit us to remark, that our business experience with women, has, perhaps, been more extensive than that of any other writer, and, therefore, some allowance must be made for the bluntness of expressions pertaining to what we so lamentably *know*. We have discovered that the most common error of the women of the present day, is that of looking for happiness somewhere outside of useful work. But we are very confident that it has never yet been found when thus sought, and never will be while the world stands; and the louder this truth is proclaimed, the better for our sex. If any doubt the truth of our assertions, let them glance around among their female acquaintances, and select those who appear to have the most enjoyment in life. Are they Idlers and Dissimulators, or are they honest workers? we know what the *answer* will be. Of all miserable human beings it has been our fortune or misfortune to know, they are the most wretched who have retired from useful employment in order to enjoy themselves, or those who never had any useful occupation. And as to "opinion"—it is surely better to be looked upon as an honest though humble *laborer* than to have enemies winking and blinking behind your back, with hints as to "how she can live and dress so, when she has neither income nor any occupation." But, pray, excuse us. Our book is nearly completed. A few pages more, and then we are done.

* * * * *

The clergyman's wife was called away to heaven, ere their daughter attained her eighteenth year, and his heart was full of affliction. But instead of twining himself around his daughter all the closer, now that he was so desolate, and she so lonely, he took to his closet, and studied and read gloomy books for consolation, leaving her to find sympathy as best she could. A little while longer, and she loved a man quite odious to the sight of her father. He was dissipated and wild; but she loved him just as obstinately and headstrong as daughters always do when they take a notion, and, in defiance of her father's angry injunctions, and the warning looks of the neighbors, she would marry the man of her heart, and so, marry him she did. Then the clergyman said: "Get thee gone! Thou hast seriously offended me, and I will own thee no longer."

"Pooh! What care I?" flouted the daughter. "Haven't I got a husband?"

The clergyman buried himself still deeper

in the dusty pages of his gloomy books, and went on preaching the gospel, but he prayed no more for his disobedient daughter. She went away with her husband, and he never heard her voice again.

* * * * * * * *

One cold winter day, two boys saw a dead body floating in the North river. The tide had nearly carried it past the city, when the agents of the law fastened a rope to one of its limbs and drew it ashore.

A paragraph in the newspapers told the world that the body of a beautiful young woman was found drowned, and many curious people went to the dead-house with anxious faces.

Days elapsed, and as no one claimed the body, the undertaker was bidden to carry it away.

"I should like to know her history," said an old man, with white hair, a stranger, who last came to view the body.

"Dare say," was the keeper's gruff reply. "Everybody likes to know all about these hidden things, though they're not always satisfied, I reckon."

"Pray remove the cloth from her face," said the stranger, apparently heedless of the keeper's words. "I wish to see how the poor creature looks."

"Dare say. Everybody likes to see. Can't do it, though. Got orders to nail her up. Been here long enough for all them to see her as wanted to. So in goes the nails, and look out for the hammer."

"Stay!" insisted the stranger, catching the keeper by the arm, and looking him straight in the face. "I ask only a moment's delay. You can give me a glimpse of her features."

"Dare say. But can't and *shan't!*"

"Hold!" exclaimed the venerable man, who seemed very resolute in his purpose. "I *must* see it before you nail the lid on—understand, I *must!*" As he spoke, he turned quite pale, and the muscles of his face twitched in nervous tremor.

"Dare say," retorted the keeper, in a harsh tone, with a leer. "If you want to see it, you ken go and dig it up, after it's buried. But you don't see it now, unless you're stronger nor I be. So take advice, and stand off."

"*Will* you grant the favor I ask?" again urged the stranger.

"*Out* of my way, old chap!—haven't I said NO?"

"Then I will do it myself!" said the stranger, suddenly jerking the corner of the cloth. His eyes saw the ghastly visage, and with a cry of horror he sank to the floor.

* * * * * * * *

Do you see that old man kneeling there in prayer? And would you know why he is thus appealing to Heaven? We will tell you. He is the clergyman of whom we have been writing, and he is there upon his knees beside a rude coffin in the dead-house, where he found the sad remains of his daughter. He is full of grief, and now frantically appeals to God that beyond the grave, there may be a place of rest for the departed. And now, when it is too late, he sees the error of having sacrificed the soul of his only child in his over zeal to save the souls of his congregation.

THE END.

Voyages and Travels,	Original Tales,	Select Literary Gems,
How to Cook Well,	How to Live Well,	How to Talk,
How to Behave,	Precepts for Parents,	Examples for Children,
What to Wear,	Art of Dressing,	Amateur Gardening,
New Inventions,	New Discoveries,	Lessons for Youth,
Tales & Biographies,	Family Pastimes,	Rules for Living,
Needle Work,	Advice to Mothers,	Hints to Young Ladies,
Puzzles and Enigmas,	Travels & Adventures,	Science & Philosophy,
Remarkable Oddities,	Notes on Fashions,	General Information,
Domestic Stories,	Scenes in Social Life,	Hints to Manufacturers
Hints to Mechanics,	Hints to Merchants,	Hints to Farmers,
Advice to Doctors,	Advice to Lawyers,	Wise Sayings,
Original Items,	Lectures for Girls,	Facts for Everybody,
&c.,	&c.,	&c.

☞ And ILLUSTRATED with

☞ NUMEROUS ENGRAVINGS.

SUBSCRIPTION ALWAYS IN ADVANCE.

One Copy, One Year,	75 cts	One Copy, Sixteen Months,	$1.
" " Six Months,	42 "	Five Copies, One Year,	$3.
" " Three Months,	25 "	Ten Copies, One Year,	$5.

☞ For a remittance of $4 we will send SIX COPIES of the paper ONE YEAR, and one copy of "**Women of New York,**" the latter as a Premium, free of postage.

☞ Bills of any solvent Bank, or United States Postage Stamps, may be sent in a letter, by mail. But DRAFTS are much safer, and if drawn PAYABLE TO OUR ORDER, they may be sent at OUR risk.

☞ Postage only Six Cents a Year, payable where the papers are received.

☞ Delivered in New York City, below 40th street, FREE of postage.

☞ Subscribers in the British Provinces must each send Six Cents in money or United States Stamps, to PRE-PAY EXTRA postage.

☞ Enclose Six Cents or Two red United States Stamps for Specimen Copy, and address

MARIE LOUISE HANKINS & CO.,

"FAMILY NEWSPAPER" Office,

NEW YORK CITY.

www.ingramcontent.com/pod-product-compliance
Lightning Source LLC
LaVergne TN
LVHW010152110826
845151LV00002B/496
* 9 7 8 1 4 2 5 5 3 8 1 1 8 *